MANUFACTURING
DELUSION

MANUFACTURING DELUSION

How the Left Uses
Brainwashing, Indoctrination,
and Propaganda Against You

Buck Sexton

Sentinel

Sentinel
An imprint of Penguin Random House LLC
1745 Broadway, New York, NY 10019
penguinrandomhouse.com

SENTINEL and SENTINEL with lantern design are registered trademarks of Penguin Random House LLC.

Most Sentinel books are available at a discount when purchased in quantity for sales promotions or corporate use. Special editions, which include personalized covers, excerpts, and corporate imprints, can be created when purchased in large quantities. For more information, please call (212) 572-2232 or e-mail specialmarkets@penguin randomhouse.com. Your local bookstore can also assist with discounted bulk purchases using the Penguin Random House corporate Business-to-Business program. For assistance in locating a participating retailer, e-mail B2B@penguinrandomhouse.com.

Book design by Alissa Rose Theodor

Library of Congress Control Number: 2025037612
ISBN 9780593716588 (hardcover)
ISBN 9780593716595 (ebook)

Printed in the United States of America
1st Printing

The authorized representative in the EU for product safety and compliance is Penguin Random House Ireland, Morrison Chambers, 32 Nassau Street, Dublin D02 YH68, Ireland, https://eu-contact.penguin.ie.

Contents

MANUFACTURING
DELUSION

Introduction

2005, Northern Nigeria

At first, it felt good when I told the head of my CIA office that I'd "go anywhere the mission needs me" for my first tasking abroad. But I started to regret it as soon as I got off the plane and felt that first blast of equatorial heat. I was twenty-three, a new trainee, and wanted to be useful to the Agency mission as soon as possible. We were still in the early days of the Global War on Terror, and I wanted to do my part. Perhaps management decided to teach me some humility and send me where nobody else in the office wanted to go. And so here I was, maneuvering through the teeming slums of northern Nigeria in a part of Africa that very few Westerners—or really any outsiders at all—ever visit. Why would they? It was an inhospitable, dangerous place.

Yet this remote corner of Africa had attracted the attention of the counterterrorism world. For months, there had been sketchy intelligence reports—"raw, unverified intelligence" in Agency parlance—that a global terrorist organization was looking to establish roots here. Whatever I thought of the assignment, the US government had reasons for sending me and a team of more senior officers to investigate.

I followed my minder—a member of Nigeria's secret police—as we walked upon wooden planks across small streams of raw sewage. None of the thousands of simple corrugated-metal roof shanties around me had indoor plumbing. Sewage was dumped from buckets into the street. The smell, as you may imagine, was unbearable.

Back at Langley, I'd done enough research on this part of Nigeria to know that it was one of the poorest, most treacherous places on earth. Simply drinking the wrong water could mean contracting Guinea worm, a nightmarish parasite that slowly burrows out of the host and can cause blindness in humans if the victim is unlucky enough to have the parasite exit through an eye.

Severe diseases, like polio, that had been eradicated in most of the world were still breaking out here. In fact, at the time of my visit, a strain of avian flu had caused an epidemic. I will never forget when, flanked by two members of the secret police, I was awakened by one of them as we drove through some ramshackle chicken farm, with a degree of excitement, to tell me, "Mr. James, we are now passing the site of the first bird flu."

But I wasn't there on a mission from the World Health Organization to track a viral epidemic. I was a junior CIA analyst on seemingly a wild-goose chase to determine if the first cases of a psychological pandemic—jihadism—were breaking out. Sketchy reports hit my computer back at Langley that an emissary from al-Qaeda had taken up residence in this forsaken region and was establishing ties to local imams and other radicals. There were even fragments captured through intelligence collection about this operative's desire to set up terror training camps—just like what al-Qaeda had established previously in Afghanistan. The mere mention of any of this at Langley created tense fights among analysts. Some thought it was all nonsense. Others believed it was the germ of a movement that could become a vortex of terrorist violence and pose a threat to the whole region.

Years later, the latter group was proved right.

The secret police walked me around the slum as small children gathered around me in a group. Even very young girls— seven or eight years old—were dressed in head-to-toe, jet-black Islamic garb, with only their faces showing. I expected something like this in Saudi Arabia, but not in Nigeria.

My minders told me that for the youngest ones, it was unlikely they'd ever seen a white person up close before, or if they had, it was only medical personnel from the NGOs that operated in the area. I was a curiosity—a young American, flanked with armed police, speaking to locals. Clearly sticking out, I was followed by a crowd, stepping carefully over streams of raw sewage that crisscrossed the muddy pathways between houses.

My secret police guides told me the area was ripe for jihadist infiltration and recruitment. They wanted us to get word back to Langley that this area needed more resources from Western partners and attention from the international community to prevent radicalization. They took me past a mosque that their informants claimed was espousing the most radical, anti-Western (and specifically anti-Christian) rhetoric and calling for violence. Even though the security agents with me had full arrest authority, they didn't want to move on the imam because they worried that to do so would spark conflict that could spiral out of control.

Then they took me around a corner to see dozens of young boys (only boys) sitting on the ground next to a cement block structure that provided some shade from the brutal midday sun.

"What are they doing?" I asked one of my guides.

"This is school for them. It's madrassa. They are learning Allah's word," he answered. There was no math or reading or traditional Western education. They were being taught the Koran, in Arabic. And, as it turned out, money from the Gulf Arab states was pouring into the country. Except when it came to the oil in the south of the country, the West had forgotten this corner of Africa—but the Islamist states of the Middle East had other ideas. There were delusions manufactured in service of a vast jihadist conspiracy.

After a few weeks in the country, I returned to Langley to write up an assessment of the terrorism risk in the area. But it didn't make any impact. I was too junior and nowhere near an expert in the region. Plus, the case that jihadism could ever spread to West Africa would require a lot more evidence—and casualties—before getting serious attention. Along with the assessments of many junior analysts before me, my write-up was relegated to a few shelved manila folders marked SECRET, stored on a classified hard drive.

But the story was just beginning.

Humanity's Greatest Threat

I didn't realize the extent of it at the time, but in West Africa I had been exposed to ground zero of a psychic epidemic. The early warning signs of radicalism were clear—hateful rhetoric, a steady diet of propaganda instead of education, teaching kids mindless repetition of the Islamist line—and soon enough violent mass hysteria would spread throughout the region. Over the course of a decade, this area would rank among the most violent terror hot spots on the planet. To this day, the jihadist conflict in Nigeria rages in the form of an ongoing religious war that has taken thousands of lives and plunged the nation into chronic instability.

But at the time I visited, the seeds of jihadism being planted in Africa were far from our first concern. When I returned to America, it was clear the Iraq War was spiraling out of control. In 2006, the CIA director—known as the "Seventh Floor" at Langley—put out a call to any and all Agency officers: If you want to surge to Iraq and an Iraq-focused element will take you, nobody internally can stop the move. Pushing the bureaucracy aside like this was a rarity. We all knew what was going on: America was on the cusp of losing the Iraq War. Anyone who wanted to raise their hand and help was to be given that opportunity.

I raised my hand.

Soon I found myself on a military base in Mosul. It all felt a little surreal to be out there, "down range." I made my way to a war zone and found myself looking over the cityscape of Mosul each morning outside the base, drinking coffee and occasionally hearing the resounding boom of an enemy suicide car-bomber ambush or the *thump-thump-thump* of our military's .50-caliber machine guns returning fire from Humvees.

I lived for months on a base with elite Special Operations warriors, but my role was intelligence collection and analysis—primarily assisting with targeting al-Qaeda in Iraq (AQI). AQI were brutal Islamist fanatics who would give their lives to murder others on the pathway to paradise and seventy-two virgins. They specialized in car bombing, head chopping, and all manner of sadistic mayhem. But these "holy warriors" also operated like a mafia entity, fixated on kidnapping, extortion, and other illicit ways of getting money. They derived glee from torture and made regular beheading videos, which they would put out on the internet to terrify the world. I'd spent months at Langley reading cable traffic about horrific AQI suicide bombings at crowded markets. By the time I arrived, the country was being pulled apart in sectarian warfare, as Shia militia members engaged in reprisal killings. Some of these involved public executions in broad daylight with chainsaws and power drills to execute Sunnis—fellow Muslims—whom they pulled off buses or kidnapped from their cars.

How could anyone commit such evil? During my years as an analyst, I became obsessed with answering this question. They didn't become evil because of poverty or lack of education. It was belief. Many al-Qaeda militants were once normal people. Some of their leaders were even high-functioning professionals with university degrees. They were reasonably intelligent people who professed to be religious Muslims— mujahideen, or holy warriors—but they were certain in their belief that Allah condoned murder, rape, and genocide.

Because of groups like AQI, Iraq was in the grip of madness.

If West Africa had the first symptoms of a psychological epidemic, Iraq was the full-blown virus. From my post as an analyst in Mosul, and later in Baghdad and Kabul, I saw over and over the repeating pattern of once-normal people transforming into bloodthirsty killers. We weren't just fighting people armed with bombs and guns. We were fighting a psychological virus. As the years passed, it became clear that the United States could not save the Middle East from the epidemics of belief that were ravaging it.

Threat Intelligence

Mass delusions rooted in false belief have roiled the Middle East time and again. But we would be foolish to think we're immune here in the West. In 2021, a decade after I left Kabul, I, like all Americans, was confronting a surge of restrictions based in mob mania. I was living in Manhattan, where I'd returned home after my time in the Agency, but everyone was in the same boat. Beginning in 2020, Covid, a viral pandemic, had triggered a psychic pandemic. Stores were closed, businesses were shut down, masks were mandated, and private citizens began being tracked in the name of "contract tracing."

Then, only a few months after the first case appeared in the United States, the death of George Floyd would ignite an all-consuming, countrywide "racial reckoning."

Protesting turned to rioting all summer, and Manhattan—already paralyzed by fear of Covid—turned dystopic as looters smashed windows and grabbed luxury goods from stores. Leftist politicians and prosecutors, both in New York and around the country, punished law enforcement instead of the criminals. In this fun house, being "antiracist" required being soft on crime; systemic racism was seen as a bigger threat than getting knifed on the New York City subway. And suddenly, the health experts decided the risks of mass gatherings were well worth it, Covid be damned.

As the collective psychosis of lockdowns for the law abiding and looting for lawbreakers took hold of the United States, I realized that whether it's in a war zone rife with jihadists or here at home during a pandemic, the biggest threat to humanity is mass delusion. Normal, educated people can be convinced that right is wrong, that up is down, that silence is violence, and that violence is justified (when done for the "right" reasons and by the "right" people).

Now, as a civilian, my career is dedicated to understanding how these delusions infiltrate civilizations, take hold, and destroy them. I began learning as much as I could, supplementing what I'd already learned in the Agency with the history of mind control stretching over the last hundred-plus years as well as the thinking of groundbreaking journalists, psychologists, and psychiatrists such as Edward Hunter, Robert Jay Lifton, and Joost

Meerloo, respectively. I began sharing what I'd learned with my audience of millions on my nationally syndicated radio program, *The Clay Travis and Buck Sexton Show*.

Now I've assembled everything I've learned into a book so that anyone can learn to spot mass delusion before it spirals out of control. History proves that if mass delusion overcomes a population, a descent into madness can be quite rapid. The distance from liberal democracy to autocratic dystopia can be measured in just a few short years. Often it happens so fast that those who are otherwise sharp social observers miss the warning signs. And as delusion comes from within the mind, it all begins with individual mind control. Adding together hundreds—of millions—of those in grip of mind control creates mass delusion. This is not a random process. There are tactics—a playbook of mind control honed by the most despotic regimes for the last one hundred years—that can transform a normal person into a brainwashed automaton.

Indeed, many people around the world have submitted to states of mass psychosis that devolved into full-blown totalitarianism. For example, the psychopathic North Korean Kim dynasty endures to this day. The foundation of that hellish nation-state—mandatory veneration of the Kim family—is a mass delusion. While North Korea menaces its neighbors and bristles with nuclear missiles, it remains too poor and backward to feed itself. But the fact that its leader remains in power is a reminder to the world that even today a state founded on mass delusion remains possible.

Just next door, another troubling totalitarianism overshadows the Kim dynasty. With China, the population was once consumed by the cult of Mao and his Cultural Revolution. Now a Communist apparatus controls the second-largest country by population—and second-largest economy—in the world. It grows in power with each passing decade. For all the protestations of the global elites that it's a "market-driven, command economy," it's also a techno-despotism with concentration camps and a recent history of mass sterilization. It has harnessed the technological advances of the last thirty years to create the most sophisticated, sweeping, and oppressive surveillance state in world history.

Added to those risks are advances in mind control–enabling technology that were unimaginable even two generations ago. Mass media—radio in particular—were necessary tools for widespread propaganda that emerged during the First World War. We're now far beyond that, living in a digital internet era of information overload and constant connectivity. Artificial intelligence means that the very evidence upon which we base our truth will be subject to distortions that can replace reality. Apart from the beneficial advances in convenience and productivity that AI brings, the implications for mind control and mass hysteria create civilizational risks that will only grow.

Tools of propaganda and information warfare are necessary for mass delusion. But tools alone can't deceive people. People deceive people—and often deceive themselves. History tells us that the seeds of totalitarianism are sometimes planted long before a dictator rises. For example, in the 1930s, countless otherwise upstanding German citizens convinced themselves that the Nazis were bettering society despite their vicious bigotry. Well-educated Soviet and Chinese Communists believed their utopian goals justified genocide during the Great Purge and Great Famine, respectively. In each case, people believed they were doing good by committing evil. The ideological atrocities of the twentieth century that killed hundreds of millions and enslaved billions were man-made catastrophes that all shared a single trait: the triumph of mass psychosis.

Don't think it can't happen here. Germany gave us Beethoven. Russia gave us Tolstoy. China gave us Confucius. At various points in history the Middle East was a global center of art, philosophy, and culture. Yet at some point every one of these places went crazy. Anyone who thinks that a society cannot collectively go insane has neither read nor understood the history of our species. The totalitarian mindset is a mass delusion. It is also a contagious mental illness that can affect any of us.

But mass delusion doesn't spread naturally—at least not at first. People don't turn from doctors into chainsaw-wielding psychopaths just because. Psychological epidemics are created through an exploitative machinery that assaults the mind. It's not natural; it's *manufactured*.

The types of delusions that infect populations vary in style and intensity. Sometimes it's the cult worship of the Kim dynasty in North Korea. Other times it's the ethnic hatred of the Nazis or the religious animosity of the jihadists. With the Soviets and the Chinese Communists, the delusion was based on class warfare. In America the delusions prey upon our good nature—our desire to keep others safe from Covid or to rectify past racial injustices.

In each case the tactics used to foment mass delusion—also called mass formation psychosis or mass hysteria—differ. Likewise, different types of mass delusion have different intensities and levels of destruction—though delusions have a way of spiraling out of control quickly.

While the approaches and tactics may differ, all manufactured delusions have one thing in common: They are rooted in lies. Sometimes they are lies about the nature of societal problems. For the Nazis, every societal ill was caused by the Jews; for the Soviets, it was the bourgeoisie. Other times, they're lies about human nature. For example, one of the greatest mass delusions in the West today is that people can change their gender. To be sure, mass delusions are not simply collective error. They're not simply "getting it wrong." It's only a mass delusion if it has been proved false—yet people believe it anyway. The provision of contrary evidence, no matter how clear, only enrages them. The delusion becomes sacred.

Likewise, those who manufacture delusion are united by the same ultimate goal: power. When people are stripped of the ability to think and act for themselves, unable to see the world clearly or to distinguish truth from fiction, they can be manipulated and controlled by people in power.

When infected with delusions, once-free people can become bitter, violent, and destructive slaves—and they won't even know it happened. People become the enemies of their own freedom and civilization.

Once mass delusion takes hold, it is extremely difficult to end. But if identified and countered early, it can be nipped in the bud. My aim in this book is to equip you with an understanding of the tactics used to foment mass delusion. I've combed through the last hundred-plus years of literature on the topic of mass delusion and identified the eight most common tactics totalitarians use to create it: conditioning, menticide, brainwashing, weaponized law, forced phobia, isolation, identity construction, and propaganda. While, as we will see, some of these tactics bleed into one another (and totalitarians rarely, if ever, use just one), each has been distinctly deployed and used both in history and today.

And knowing how they are used is vital. When we can see

how the enemy works, we can begin to fight back against the false beliefs that can lead to disastrous consequences.

But where to begin?

Manufacturing delusion requires the takeover of minds. There is always a process at work—a series of tactics applied over time that result in extreme obedience.

This kind of mind control has a name: conditioning.

1

Conditioning

Manhattan, New York, 2020

The early days of the Covid pandemic in NYC were surreal: empty streets that were eerily silent except for wailing ambulances, exhaust from the refrigerated morgue trucks parked outside hospitals, people looking on warily from their balconies (if they were lucky enough to have one). I watched from my home radio studio as the US naval hospital ship *Comfort* sailed into New York Harbor. Friends were sending me photos of tents erected in Central Park to serve as a field hospital for Covid overflow. New Yorkers were desperate and afraid.

New York—like pretty much all of America—was locked down. People were hiding in their apartments. Public transit was empty. When anyone did go out, they made sure to keep a "safe" distance from everyone else.

It was easy to understand the fear at the beginning. Confusing reports from China, Italy, and—soon enough—everywhere around the world indicated that this virus was fast-spreading and deadly. People naturally responded based on their fear of the worst.

Within a few months we had a lot more data and started to learn a startling fact: The disease really wasn't that deadly at all. Aside from some particularly high-risk populations, the worst most people would get were symptoms similar to those of a really rough cold before moving on with their lives.

But that didn't stop the pandemic restrictions from continuing for years. Even today, five years later, you can still see signs in some stores or on a jet bridge warning people to stand six feet apart. A certain percentage of the population, apparently, will never stop wearing masks.

What gives? Covid lockdowns, social distancing, and masking didn't continue long past their expiration date because of the disease. They continued because people were afraid. Rather, they were *trained* to be afraid. How? Through a process we generally call conditioning—repetitive stimuli, directed to create a physiological or psychological response—which is rooted in laboratory findings pioneered in Russia more than a century ago.

The Science of Mind Control

The Soviet leadership—first under Lenin, then Stalin—desperately wanted to create the perception that their workers' paradise was rooted in science. To bolster the narrative of the Soviet Union as a science-based utopia, they leveraged the reputation of their most famous scientist.

That scientist was Ivan Pavlov.

Dr. Ivan Pavlov was a known quantity in his field long before the rise of Soviet totalitarianism. In 1904, he received a Nobel Prize "in recognition of his work on the physiology of digestion."[1] But he is best known today as the founding father of an area of behaviorism known as classical conditioning, based in what he called the "conditional reflex." We use the term *conditioning* today to refer to any training or programming that pushes an animal or human to react in a predetermined way. But for Dr. Ivan Pavlov, conditional reflex was something much more specific—and, at the time, revolutionary.

Pavlov performed his experiments on animals. In a laboratory setting he had been able to induce a physiological reaction in dogs—salivation—in response to a stimulus (usually a buzzer or metronome) that had regularly indicated food was coming. Through associating the buzzer with food, the dogs' brains had been conditioned to salivate at the sound of the buzzer, whether or not food was present.

But could this sort of conditioning go beyond the mechanistic salivation reflex and change voluntary behaviors of the dogs? Pavlov began to wonder.

In 1924, Pavlov accidentally stumbled upon an answer when his laboratory in Leningrad (present-day Saint Petersburg) was severely flooded during a storm. The dogs Pavlov kept for his experiments nearly drowned but were saved at the last moment by members of Pavlov's research staff who burst into the facility. While the dogs survived, they were never the same—and Dr. Pavlov noted major behavioral changes in them.

After the flood, the dogs' previous conditioning was suddenly wiped away. Dogs who once loved certain members of Pavlov's staff, for instance, now showed aggression toward them. The trauma of the flood seemed to have reprogrammed the dogs. Pavlov began to wonder about the implications of this event. If dogs could be reprogrammed so completely, could humans?

While Pavlov found that conditioning humans wouldn't be so simple, his discovery of the conditional reflex was a first scientific step toward understanding how to manipulate human behavior. He committed himself to exploring the recesses of the human mind based on both underlying anatomy and outside stimuli. And while his findings were limited, he concluded that external stimuli can trigger human reflex reactions as well.[2]

A confounding variable that Pavlov struggled to solve over

decades was that his canine subjects had traits innate to them—personalities, in essence—that could dramatically affect their conditional response. And he knew that if this was true for dogs, things would be even more complicated for human beings.

Coincidentally, while Pavlov was making groundbreaking discoveries and becoming the most famous Russian scientist of all time, the Soviet Union began to form its totalitarian apparatus obsessed with absolute control of society through dominating their minds.

The Soviets took notice of Pavlov's work. What better tool could a tyrannical regime have than a system to control minds by inducing reflexive psychological responses?

Politically, Lenin, Stalin, and other Soviet leaders claimed to be leveraging Pavlov's genius to advance their dictatorship of the proletariat. This pretense of a scientifically-driven society gave their Marxist planning a veneer of legitimacy.

While the Soviets were happy to commandeer Pavlov's reputation at first, they were not so kind to Pavlov himself. In the early years after the October Revolution, Pavlov was a victim of the brutish, blundering Soviet system. He even went through a period of extreme deprivation when his lab fell into disrepair and he struggled to find food. He fed his family in part with a garden he had planted himself. Eventually, though, Lenin realized the value Pavlov brought to the new Soviet project, and extended him financial support to conduct his research. Thus,

Pavlov had what biographer Daniel Todes calls a "combative collaboration" with the Soviets. He was one of the few Soviet citizens who publicly criticized the Communists while ultimately benefiting from their state-funded largesse.

Later in his life, around his eightieth birthday, Pavlov accepted Soviet government patronage for the construction and staffing of the Koltushi complex near Leningrad. This sprawling institution, a village unto itself, would officially be called the Institute of Experimental Genetics of Higher Nervous Activity.

At Koltushi, Pavlov sought to apply the knowledge acquired from experimenting on dogs to human neurology and psychology. As Pavlov would tell the Soviet propaganda organ *Izvestia*, Koltushi had a primary mission: "Our work will result in the success of eugenics—the science of the development of an improved human type."[3]

The Soviet leadership clearly believed this was an important mission for propaganda purposes—and they hoped much more. Vyacheslav Molotov, the head of the Council of People's Commissars, called the creation of Koltushi a top priority for the Soviet government. (Pavlov's scientific goals at Koltushi were ambitious, but he didn't get very far with them. He would have only a few years at Koltushi before dying in 1936.)

Despite the privileges the Soviet regime afforded him, Pavlov was a rare outspoken critic of its failures—one who would never face the wrath of the gulag or firing squad. In 1924, speaking in the City Duma's great hall on Nevskii Prospekt, Pavlov stood in front of the room and slammed not just the politics of the revolution but the Russian people's inability to see reality. Pavlov diagnosed it in scientific terms, as paraphrased by Todes:

> The suppression of private property and persecution of religion had profoundly shaken Russians' nervous system, causing a mass neurotic "breakdown" characterized by "tendencies to succumb to fantastic suggestions." Having always suffered from an imbalance between excitation and inhibition, Russians were now totally incapable of seeing things as they really were. Their reflexes "are coordinated, not with reality, but with words."[4]

Pavlov was often despondent over what the October Revolution had done to his country and its people. He recognized that his native Russia was undergoing a mass psychosis under Soviet rule. Even as the regime was flailing from population-wide starvation and failed five-year plans, many of its people still believed against all odds in the promises of Communism. The suffering, as horrific as it was, would lead them to a workers' paradise.

Despite his criticism of the regime, Pavlov would eventually become a prized symbol for the Soviets, leveraged by Stalin's inner circle for international prestige. At the highest level, the Soviets would decide to protect Pavlov—and even give him considerable resources to expand his work. Part of Pavlov hoped that the Soviets would improve their ability to govern, and he also felt he owed it to his countrymen as well as science to continue his research.

Under Soviet Communism, the Russian people were forced into a mass delusion. The entire Soviet apparatus became a massive mind-control machine that combined constant psychological terror with extreme violence. Ironically, Pavlov discovered conditional reflex in the same era that the Soviet Union began a decades-long experiment in totalitarian conditioning, with devastating human costs.

Stalin relentlessly proclaimed himself a defender of the people while ordering the deaths of millions. Dissidents were tortured until they gave Party-approved answers and confessions—or until they died. For instance, during the Moscow trials of the 1930s, the Soviets used torture as an extreme stimulus—including smashing toes and ribs—to force confessions from innocent prisoners. While the threat of force was constant, even absent actual violence, psychological terror in the Soviet Union was omnipresent. Like Pavlov conditioning his dogs to salivate when there was no food, people were forced to say agricultural production was up while store shelves were empty, conditioned to not believe their lying eyes. Even their minds weren't allowed to be free.

Over years of relentless and brutal conditioning, many came to believe the most obvious lies from the regime.

After Pavlov died in 1936, his legend continued to be a tool the Soviet apparatus wielded to its benefit. Stalin embraced the concepts of Pavlov and, around 1949, "heralded a Pavlovian revolution in the Soviet behavioral sciences. The principle of the conditioned reflex was made the basis of a new Soviet concept of man," according to Robert C. Tucker.[5]

Fortunately, Stalin was never able to take Pavlov's findings and transform them into some science fiction ray gun that could wipe and reprogram the minds of the masses. As time went on, it became abundantly clear that the Soviet Union was more reliant upon brute force than on the trained submission of the masses. The people could be conditioned to live in fear and keep silent—and for decades that was enough to maintain control. But in the end, they could not be conditioned to really believe in the mass delusions of the Soviet Union.

Despite its eventual failure, the Soviet experiment in mass conditioning had enormous impact beyond its boundaries. It provided a template for other totalitarian approaches, such as in China and North Korea.

On a far less extreme level, there are even some efforts at

mass conditioning in liberal democracies, including here in the United States.

Indeed, this collision of science, politics, and mass conditioning continues today. Physical stimuli are manipulated to generate responses in the brain that may be subconscious. This is done to establish control. In a recent tragicomic episode of this phenomenon, a far less eminent scientist than Pavlov would go so far as to call the policies that conditioned Americans to ignore the real evidence surrounding a very different crisis "*the* science."

His name is Dr. Anthony Fauci.

The Covid System of Control

Anthony Fauci—then director of the National Institute of Allergy and Infectious Diseases—wasn't the only public health leader relentlessly pushing the most extreme and damaging responses to the pandemic in 2020 and beyond. Sadly, extremism was in abundant supply when a new coronavirus started rapidly spreading through the world. But, based on his position as an adviser to the president and as the face of the Covid response, Fauci, more than any other figure, conditioned Americans to adopt a mass delusion. Perhaps the biggest sign of that delusion? Convincing everyone in America to wear a surgical mask to "slow the spread."

It quickly became obvious that mass mask wearing didn't slow the spread of infection, and numerous studies later confirmed that fact. Even Dr. Fauci knew that masking would be useless in preventing or slowing transmission. "Masks are really for infected people to prevent them from spreading infection to people who are not infected rather than protecting uninfected people from acquiring infection,"[6] he wrote the former secretary of Health and Human Services on February 5, 2020.

He confirmed the idea that the masks worn by most of the public didn't help much at the end of the pandemic. "From a broad public-health standpoint, at the population level, masks work at the margins—maybe 10 percent,"[7] he told an interviewer in April 2023. It turned out, that estimate was too high. A Cochrane study—considered the gold standard in the medical community for weighing scientific evidence—came out in 2023 stating that, based on all the scientifically rigorous studies available, masking offered no statistically provable effect on Covid mitigation and makes "little or no difference."[8]

In hindsight, one begins to wonder whether slowing the spread was ever the point. Rather, masks functioned like a conditioning tool, a symbol of obedience to the regime. They made us fearful—fearful of others. They made us easier to control. We wore them even though they made breathing hard, human interaction difficult, and eating comedic. And we now know that masks intrude on the autonomic nervous system. They can also elevate blood pressure and heartbeat and have a range of effects on the mind.

We were told, despite all the evidence, that masking was about "trusting the science." In fact, it was about trusting the *scientists*. It was not about following the facts but conditioning us to be obedient to the ruling class.

If this was about following the science, we would have heeded the fact that the Centers for Disease Control and Prevention (CDC) knew as early as September 2020 that Covid was spreading by aerosol transmission. They acknowledged this fact on their website only to take it right off.[9] The World Health Organization (WHO) also resisted admitting until August 2020 that aerosol transmission was a factor, and kept downplaying it even when they had to adjust.[10]

Why does this matter? Because an aerosol virus could not be stopped by public health's command-and-control playbook. Instead, the CDC—flexing in this Super Bowl of pandemics—ordered everyone to wear a mask on public transportation in January 2021.[11] The White House didn't acknowledge aerosol spread until March 2022.[12] Even then, the Biden administration continued to enforce the CDC's oppressive mask mandate until it was struck down by a court in April 2022.[13]

The whole mask madness was theater. But this was never acknowledged by the public health establishment, even after it was repeatedly demonstrated by the evidence during and after the pandemic.

Like every group infected with totalitarian impulses, when public health authorities were proved wrong, they dug in more. If one mask didn't work, we were told to wear two. If they couldn't make you believe in it on practical grounds, many of the top politicians and pundits pushed masking on moral grounds ("if you don't mask, you'll kill Grandma!").

Yet those same people were constantly caught violating masking protocols. They didn't appear to believe their own lies, but they demanded we obey. Donning a mask when we walked into a store, sat in a restaurant, or got near another person could subconsciously stimulate in our brain a Covid fear response. The mask mandates perpetuated the mass delusions that gripped our society during the pandemic.

But masking was not the only Covid-era conditioning tactic. In March 2020, the CDC announced a policy of "social distancing" to "slow the spread" of Covid. This was initially justified as necessary to protect the capacity of the US health-care system from a sudden surge of cases, leaving the most critically ill patients without care. The social-distancing policy would eventually shift, without explanation, to a semi-permanent cultural and social practice, entirely untethered to preserving health care capacity. For years, social distancing meant closing public gathering places, strictly limiting group events, and encouraging people to avoid human contact as much as possible.

Most absurd of all, the health authorities came up with a specific measure—six feet—as the marker of relative safety from other human beings. There were never any meaningful data to back up this specific distance. Over time, public health officials backed down from this advice. Fauci himself later admitted the six-foot rule was effectively made up.[14]

Even so, social distancing became the basis for some of the most restrictive public-policy decisions in living memory. Outdoor playgrounds were shut down in cities across the country, even though it was known that the spread of Covid in fresh outdoor air was almost impossible. Public places, including restaurants and classrooms, were filled with plexiglass dividers. While it was immediately obvious that these movable walls were useless to stop the spread of the virus, actual scientific studies of aerodynamics would show that these walls prevented natural airflow and made infection indoors *more likely* to occur.[15]

Again, it's not like everyone was doing their best with limited information and only later realized that the science was wrong. The "science" behind masking and social distancing never passed muster, and scientists and public health "experts" knew that—or at least should have known that—from the start. These policies did not slow the spread, but they succeeded in making us paranoid.

The only indisputable benefit of social distancing is that, by the summer of 2020, we saw that it was a farce merely being used as a political cudgel. Our collective epiphany shattering the pretense of "the science" came with the Black Lives Matter riots that began in late May.

For months, the health policy establishment had insisted that gatherings were simply too dangerous because of the Covid risks. Weddings and funerals were canceled because the state demanded it. In blatant violation of the First Amendment, various local governments demanded that churches, synagogues, and other houses of worship be shuttered. Those who wanted to protest the actual lockdowns were told to disperse, as they allegedly posed a risk to public health (even when they were masked and held outdoors). Some localities even put limitations on the number of people allowed to gather in private homes, encouraging citizens to call the police to snitch on those who violated social-distancing rules.

Then, in May 2020, the death of George Floyd during his arrest sparked riots around the country. Like the flood in Pavlov's lab, it was as if months of careful isolation conditioning were erased—but only for certain authority-approved activities. Riots broke out across the country, in cities large and small. Tens of thousands of protesters took to the streets in New York City. And many of the same authorities who had up until that moment demanded—on pain of fines and even arrest—that

Americans cancel all large gatherings were suddenly endorsing mass gatherings.

While millions of businesses and houses of worship remained subject to mandatory government shutdowns because of social-distancing mandates, and indoor gatherings were still restricted to no more than ten people in many places, more than twelve hundred epidemiologists, doctors, public-health bureaucrats, and "community stakeholders" signed an open letter supporting the riots. With an explanation that strained credulity, "experts" told us that nationwide race riots were allowed *in the name of public health*. In one of the most jaw-dropping acts of credibility self-immolation imaginable, the twelve hundred–plus signatories to this open letter agreed that white supremacy was "a lethal public health issue."[16]

This was too much for any rational person to bear. But most people didn't actually change their behavior—at least not immediately. Masking and distancing had totally convinced the people that Covid was terrifyingly dangerous—even if it apparently wasn't dangerous for left-wing rioters for some reason. We had been trained to continue to accept unprecedented restrictions on our freedom even as criminals burned down our cities. As our stress level rose, a defeatist shame would grow in our minds.

Then, finally, it became impossible to ignore the truth: The virus was spreading despite the mandates. Luckily, we were told ad nauseam that a vaccine could finally stop the spread once and for all. On March 29, 2021, then CDC Director Rochelle Walensky proudly proclaimed on MSNBC that the CDC's data suggested that "vaccinated people do not carry the virus, don't get sick"—a claim the CDC itself walked back in the days following.[17]

It may seem odd that anyone would believe the experts at this point. But that's the nature of conditioning. A belief becomes so ingrained, it infuses the subconscious. The rejection of the truth is reflexive. If you believe one lie in the face of all evidence to the contrary—or at least act like you believe it—it becomes easier to believe another lie and then another. It was precisely because we'd been conditioned to follow masking and social-distancing rules despite the evidence that so many believed the authorities when they told us the vaccines would work. By that time, most people were already well trained to be afraid, to not think for themselves, and to do what they were told.

As a result, tens of millions of Americans lined up to get the vaccine and then the boosters, hoping they would finally be immune to the virus.

Again, this turned out to be entirely wrong—as evidenced by a July 4, 2021, outbreak among mostly vaccinated people in Provincetown, Massachusetts.[18] However, to the Democrats in charge of the Covid response (who had by then taken complete control in Washington), truth didn't matter. The next step in our Covid conditioning was already underway: mandatory vaccination.

Many people would rather forget the Biden government's vaccine policies of 2021. A "papers, please" regime of mandatory vaccines was rolled out. Thousands of people were fired from their jobs for vaccine non-compliance, including military personnel, first responders, and nurses who had been on the front lines of the pandemic.

The vaccine mandates did not end Covid, but they successfully demonized those who opted out. A December 2022 study by political science academics at a Danish university found "that vaccinated people express discriminatory attitudes towards unvaccinated individuals at a level as high as discriminatory attitudes that are commonly aimed at immigrant and minority populations. . . . National leaders and vaccinated members of the public appealed to moral obligations to increase COVID-19 vaccine uptake, but our findings suggest that discriminatory attitudes—including support for the removal of fundamental rights—simultaneously emerged."[19]

"The conflict between those who are vaccinated against COVID-19 and those who are not threatens societal cohesion as a new socio-political cleavage," Dr. Alexander Bor of Aarhus University commented. "The vaccinated clearly seem to be the ones deepening this rift."[20]

Of course, scientists were soon finding that our natural immunity developed from getting Covid gave us an even greater form of protection than what the vaccines could offer. But the Covid brain trust, with Dr. Fauci at the head, simply ignored the reality that natural immunity was stronger when it came to the virus. Those pushing the vaccine regime decided to advocate for universal vaccination instead—a position that was by no means backed up by "the science." It's perfectly reasonable to conclude, then, that they knew they were being dishonest, and they didn't care.

How did the Biden administration and Fauci get so many millions of Americans to go along with this?

Mass hysteria is fertile ground for political mobilization. This became clear during the pandemic when party affiliation turned into a proxy for belief in the most extreme Covid measures. The more left-wing a person, the more likely that person was to adhere to strict, often contradictory Covid measures. The prevailing propaganda led to widespread delusions that closely tracked party lines. In 2021, for example, *The New York Times* reported that 41 percent of Democrats believed that at least half of people who got Covid would need to be hospitalized.[21] The actual percentage was around 1 to 5 percent at the time. It would have been even lower if the hospitals providing this data had only tabulated those who were admitted *for* Covid, instead of those admitted for other reasons who also had Covid.

In the end, the mass delusions swiftly spiraled out of control.

What began with "mask up" and "social distance" turned into a tyrannical health regime of vaccine passports, social-distancing signs, mass closures, and arbitrary quarantine policies. Every aspect of society, from going to the grocery store to flying on a plane, became a conditioning tool. As late as 2023, many colleges mandated not just vaccines but booster shots.[22] By then, many people had had as many Covid infections as they had had vaccines.

This hysteria was a manufactured delusion. How else can one explain how so many otherwise normal Americans embraced medical absurdity and partisan viciousness in the name of science? And conditioning pushed the American people in the direction of that tyranny.

After my short assignment in Nigeria ended, extremism spread throughout the area. The terrorist group that had grown out of the seeds I saw being planted, Boko Haram, would go on to become one of the deadliest in the world, with 168 major attacks in Nigeria in 2011 alone, most of them ascribed to the group.[23] Boko Haram would have a particular focus on the recruitment of children into its ranks—often beginning the process by bribing them with candy to snitch on anyone in their village who criticized the group.[24] Huge numbers of older boys, called *almajiri*, were shipped off to study with Koranic teachers far from their homes. Most of them had no education beyond the Koran, nor any skills or job prospects. The conditioning of their minds for jihad became a wellspring of recruits for Boko Haram.

These kids were conditioned and radicalized in a relatively peaceful society. But years later I saw how an even more extreme form of mind control could be implemented in a much more violent environment. In Iraq, I saw a case study of a tactic whose history stretched all the way back to World War II not just to mold minds but to kill them.

The tactic? Menticide, meaning "the killing of the mind."

2

Menticide

Mosul, Iraq, 2007

"Welcome to Iraq," I remember thinking to myself as the UH-60 Black Hawk was diving to one side and the dual M240G machine guns were firing off, one after the other. It was only the second trip I'd ever taken in a helicopter—and it involved evasive maneuvers and live fire.

The war fighters on the helo with me were unfazed. For the guy from CIA's paramilitary Global Response Staff (GRS) sitting right next to me, it was just another day in Iraq. He didn't even flinch. If you've seen the movie *13 Hours*, about the terror attack and the fierce firefight that unfolded in Benghazi, you know what GRS is all about: elite warriors, drawn from the top tier of military operators, acting as personal security detail for civilians. Their mission was to keep spies like me from getting kidnapped and placed in orange pajamas in an al-Qaeda execution video. I really appreciated those guys.

Mosul—the provincial capital of Ninewa, with over a million people—was a world-class hellhole at the time of my assignment. By the numbers, it was arguably the most dangerous large city in Iraq. CIA bosses had sent me to do an in-depth security review of the whole province, focusing on Sunni Muslim insurgents who had turned the region into a maelstrom of jihad. I spent time learning from Special Forces, Kurdish allies, and anyone on the front lines who could speak to what was really going on.

The region was suffering from a psychological epidemic. It was the next phase of the widespread radicalism that I observed and analyzed in Nigeria. In Mosul, extremism had taken over. Old sectarian hatreds between Sunni and Shia Muslims and between Arab and Kurdish Iraqis had broken out into ferocious bloodletting. Terrorist factions were pouncing on those enmities and feeding a campaign of hysteria about coalition forces wanting to occupy Iraq forever. No conspiracy theory was too dark or outrageous for the insurgents to exploit in order to bring new recruits to their black banners.

Meanwhile, everyday Iraqis in Mosul were stuck in a constant loop of fear. At any moment, in any place, a bomb could go off, killing and maiming dozens. There were constant targeted assassinations and broad-daylight executions. Kidnapping and the most gruesome torture were commonplace. Beheading videos were posted online to remind Moslawis and the whole world of the menace all around them. Evil was running free in their city.

Sunni Muslim insurgent groups like AQI capitalized on the carnage. They convinced many young Iraqi men that the "Crusaders and Jews" (the jihadist pejorative for Americans) were bloodthirsty invaders who had brought ruin upon the country. If only they kicked them out—using horrific methods mostly directed against their fellow Iraqis—a *caliphate*, or religious Islamic state, could be built.

Amid a demoralized and terrorized population, insurgent groups thrived. Thousands of disaffected Sunni Arabs joined up alongside thuggish "insurgents" and committed the most heinous acts imaginable of torture and mutilation. To justify this sadism, they would cite battles from centuries ago or a *hadith*—stories about the Prophet Muhammad—taken from Islamic scripture.

I did not realize it when the helicopter first touched ground, but during my months in Iraq, I would learn what happens when mind-killing tactics, or what is known as menticide, take over in a war zone. In fact, insurgent groups used tactics similar to those employed by history's totalitarian tyrants as a means to program recruits who would become suicide bombers and to terrorize the general population. They knew that mental breakdown, confusion, and degradation were keys to recruiting new militants and keeping the general population in a state of fear.

How is such a breakdown on the human mind on such a large scale even possible? The jihadis in Iraq weren't trying something new. The practice of mind killing had been perfected and executed on a much grander scale nearly a century before by Joseph Stalin.

The Shock of Forced Confessions

Within three years of Ivan Pavlov's death in 1936, the world entered the largest armed conflict in history: World War II. Totalitarian regimes would attempt to take over the world, causing the deaths of tens of millions.

But before any battles broke out, there were indications that the Soviets were experimenting—successfully—with psychological techniques to completely break down the minds of targeted individuals. They were killing their minds before moving on to their bodies. While these mind-control techniques were directed against the masses, they were also employed on victims at the very top of the Soviet political hierarchy. The monster they created ate them, too.

One of the most memorable cases was Sergei Mrachkovsky, who, in 1936, publicly confessed to heinous crimes against the Soviet Union that he did not commit—including his involvement in a plot to kill Stalin.

It made no sense. Mrachkovsky had given his life to the

Communist cause. He had been the quintessential Marxist revolutionary. He was an old-school Bolshevik, having joined the party in 1905. His father was also a Bolshevik, and his grandfather was a member of the Southern Russian Workers Union, a pre-Bolshevik workers collective.[1] Mrachkovsky rose to prominence fighting for Bolshevik forces in Siberia during the civil war, where he was wounded in action. Historian Robert Conquest described him as "a real epitome of revolutionary boldness, born and bred to resistance."[2]

But on August 19, 1936, as the first major Stalinist show trials got underway, Mrachkovsky betrayed under oath everything he had ever held dear as a revolutionary. And like some of the other formerly esteemed Bolsheviks on trial, Mrachkovsky did not ask the court for mercy. He described himself, on the record, as a "traitor who should be shot."[3] Soon after the trial and his guilty verdict, the Communists complied with his request.

The Moscow trials were unlike any previous judicial proceedings. During Stalin's Great Purge of potential opposition, defendants confessed before the trials even began to crimes that sounded fantastical (because they were). More shocking than that was the complete psychological surrender of the accused, including self-abasement with confessions that were implausible, followed by demands for immediate execution. The men who faced these rigged trials actively humiliated themselves on their way to horrific sentences. They even seemed to believe in their own guilt, though their crimes were impossible. They couldn't have done the things they were admitting.

All of the Stalin show-trial defendants were convicted, and nearly all were executed by firing squad. A lucky few received lengthy prison sentences in the Soviet gulag, which might as well have been a death sentence in countless cases.

How did Stalin's judicial apparatus coerce so many false confessions from men who faced certain death?

The primary tactic Stalin's thugs relied on was mass murder, eradicating anyone who posed a threat to his goals. To this end, his security apparatus killed millions, first eliminating the kulaks, who were landholding independent famers. The terror of these liquidations created mass anxiety in the Soviet population, many of whom knew that they were living at the whims of a sadistic tyrant.

For those targeted by the state but not killed, torture was the tactic of choice, which was elevated to a major state enterprise. In the 1930s, the Stalinist machinery of terror used torture at a scale arguably unparalleled in human history. Soviet torture was as cruel as it was creative. The torturers took pleasure in the intricacy of the torments they inflicted. They invented new forms of interrogation called *stoika*, whereby prisoners were forced to stand on their tiptoes for hours or sometimes days.[4]

Grueling physical trials were frequently coupled with sleep deprivation. Stalin's minions had a term for the seemingly endless interrogations that police would deploy for days on end, specifically timed to break all sleep patterns: the "conveyor."[5] To add an element of randomness to it, the agents of the state would often shift the tone, timing, and the nature of the questions asked of the detainee to bring about a state of bewilderment. As a coup de grâce, the Stalinist apparatus also threatened to torture and kill the family members of the accused.

Why engage in all these tortures if execution is an option? The goal of the regime wasn't merely eliminating perceived opponents. It was to psychologically destroy the tortured men and women. If they survived and avoided a ten-year sentence in the gulag (a "tenner," as prisoners referred to it, according to Aleksandr Solzhenitsyn), they would return with their minds and bodies broken, spreading that brokenness to their family and friends back at home. Torture of this kind on an industrial scale is psychological warfare designed to foment mass delusion by utterly breaking the will of the population. In a word, it's menticide.

To be sure, the use of torture to break minds wasn't a new state tactic in the 1930s. Torture is as old as human civilization itself, as is the use of terror for political purposes. Russia specifically has a long history of it. The sixteenth century saw the rise of a terror regime under the command of Tsar Ivan IV

Vasilyevich, better known as "Ivan the Terrible." Ivan was a sadist who in the 1560s established an armed ministerial caste that reads like a precursor to Stalin's NKVD or the Nazi SS that would come hundreds of years later. Ivan's terror squad, or *oprichniki*, acted as bloodthirsty enforcers of Ivan's every whim, engaging in systematic detention and torture to terrorize civilian populations and mutilate any rivals for power.

While Ivan used his brutal secret police to enforce his whims and settle his most petty personal scores, Stalin had much grander ambitions. In 1939, Stalin's Central Committee decided that torture against detainees should become official practice because of the need to defeat "bourgeois intelligence services."[6] In reality, that meant defeating anything that could be labeled a bourgeois mindset. Stalin didn't just want his rivals' estates or to protect his power at any cost, as Ivan did. He wanted to own people's minds.

This is why the Communist security system was built atop a mountain of sadistic violence against its own people. Omnipresent threats—random, unjust, and extreme—became the foundation of the Communist state. The psychological damage from this to the Russian population cannot be overstated.

In the case of Sergei Mrachkovsky and the other doomed defendants of the show trials, torture while in custody was extreme. The Soviet security services alternated approaches, as they found that forced fatigue could sometimes be even more effective than pain in achieving mental annihilation. The eventual executions were almost guaranteed—but the apparatus wanted to psychologically break the prisoners first and to show their people and the world that nobody was above the state and that nobody was free from the state, even in their minds.

Some of the Soviet tactics may have been experimental. The apparatus wanted to see how quickly, and completely, they could kill minds and fundamentally break the spirit of the people so that they'd have no choice but to obey. Obedience would be automatic.

Stalin's show trials, then, were not really trials at all. They were ultimately intended as a public display of psychological degradation for the accused. They inspired paralyzing fear and also presented a propaganda opportunity for media organs of the state. For the shocking number of true believers within and outside the Soviet Union, they created a talking point about internal threats to the Communist revolution. After all, these men were admitting in court that they were guilty of the most heinous crimes!

But perhaps more important, the "conspirators" against Stalin were exposed as broken men, hollowed out from the inside down to their basic neurological functions. To those who understood the true nature of Stalin's regime, it was a warning against any resistance. After all, you might be willing to die fighting Stalin. But would you be willing to lose your mind?

The Science of Mind Killing

The Soviets may have been mad, but there was a method to their madness. In 1956—a few decades after Stalin began experimenting with various forms of torture to mentally break people—the Dutch psychoanalyst Joost Meerloo explained how exactly the human mind can be, metaphorically speaking, murdered. He coined the term *menticide* to describe this process of thought destruction that characterized what had happened to the Moscow show-trial defendants.

Meerloo, who himself was held prisoner by the Nazis during the Second World War, described menticide in his book *The Rape of the Mind* as an extreme form of mind control:

> Menticide is an old crime against the human mind and spirit but systematized anew. It is an organized system of psychological intervention and judicial perversion through which a powerful dictator can imprint his own opportunist thoughts upon the minds of those he plans to use and destroy. The terrorized victims finally find themselves compelled to express complete conformity to the tyrant's wishes.[7]

In a way, menticide is a method of creating a blank slate that those in power can then manipulate as they will.

Totalitarian regimes' mass application of menticide in the twentieth century was different from what humanity had seen before. Until the Soviet Union came along with its gulags and massive secret police services, no regime had been able to systematically break the minds and souls of millions of people with extreme physical and mental cruelty.

Some experts, including Meerloo, argued that Pavlov's findings on conditioning, regardless of intent, led to the menticidal tactics of Soviet Communism. The mere idea that one can subconsciously condition others to do something against their ultimate will was a shocking scientific breakthrough. The jump to full-on menticide was thus a matter of taking the root idea of conditioning to its extreme.

Pavlov (long deceased at the time of Meerloo's writing) would have rejected the suggestion that his life's work supported Soviet mind-control efforts. But the Soviets publicly treated Pavlov's work as foundational to their propaganda. The term *Pavlovian*, in common usage, would come to mean anything that involved a reflexive response of the brain to certain stimuli. A brilliant scientist's quest to understand the psyche was hijacked to pursue totalitarian obedience.

But Pavlov was just the spark. In the sprawling Soviet gulag prison system, the Communists created a machinery of mind destruction. Meerloo broke this system of menticide into four phases:

PHASE 1: Artificial breakdown and deconditioning

PHASE 2: Submission to and positive identification with
the enemy

PHASE 3: Reconditioning to the new order

PHASE 4: Liberation from the totalitarian spell[8]

PHASE 1: Artificial breakdown and deconditioning. The prisoner
is made to suffer—sometimes physically, but often mentally as
well. The former could include the application of extreme pain
through torture, sleep interruption, starvation, and exposure to
cold temperatures. The latter could include various forms of
humiliation, isolation, interrogation, and more. Meerloo noted
that torture "is intended to a much greater extent to act as a
threat to the bystanders' (the people's) imagination. Their wild
anticipation of torture leads more easily to *their* breakdown
when the enemy has need of their weakness."[9]

**PHASE 2: Submission to and positive identification with the
enemy.** The detainee enters this phase upon total surrender to
the authority in charge. The normal protective mechanisms of
rage against the injustice of the situation, hope for outside res-
cue, or the belief that the detainment is a mistake that will be
corrected all disappear. In fact, the menticide victim will begin
to agree with the captors and can even develop a fondness for

them.[10] (The Swedish psychiatrist Nils Bejerot would later dub this phenomenon "Stockholm syndrome" after what he observed in a hostage taking at a Stockholm bank in 1973.)

Drawing upon his expertise as a psychiatrist, Meerloo saw in the submission phase a deep psychological shift of the detainee in response to trauma. "What the inquisitor calls the sudden inner illumination and conversion," Meerloo writes, "is a total reversal of inner strategy in the victim." This fundamental shift in mindset creates a phenomenon that appears bizarre to an outside observer, where the victim begins to "speak his new master's voice."[11] This submission is the heart of menticide.

PHASE 3: **Reconditioning to the new order.** This is the indoctrination phase of menticide. As Meerloo writes, there is a "continuous training and taming . . . the new phonograph has to be grooved."[12] Upon the ideological carcass left behind by menticide, a new framework of belief is built. The mandated slogans and self-contradictory maxims of the new regime are firmly implanted in the mind of the victim. This stage is an individualized form of brainwashing, which we will get to in the next chapter. As I mentioned at the beginning, some of these mind-control tactics bleed together and are interrelated.

PHASE 4: **Liberation from the totalitarian spell.** Soviets often attempted to murder the mind in order to put a new mind in its place. But it doesn't always work. When a subject breaks free to normal society, there is often a process of psychological reclamation, a rebirth of reality, that takes place and occurs in phases. During this period, there will sometimes be physical manifestations, including "crying spells, feelings of guilt and depression."[13] At this point, most victims will slowly come back to reality. But in rare cases, the victim remains permanently affixed to the ideology of the enemy.

The Stalinist regime used this system of menticide millions of times over to enslave a vast nation for generations. Immoral and inhumane as it is, menticide clearly works. Even if relatively few victims permanently accepted the ideological transplant forced upon them, nobody leaves menticide the same—and everyone else is terrified that the same evil could be inflicted on them, too.

At its core, the first three stages of menticide before a probable liberation are built upon dehumanization. And that dehumanization is achieved through torture in two ways: by causing confusion and degradation.

Confusion and Degradation

To achieve menticide, the Stalinist prison system sought to undermine the neural defenses of the subject, then turn the brain toward self-hatred. A critical step in this process was to bring about a state of mental disorientation tantamount to a temporary psychosis. In *The Rape of the Mind*, Meerloo describes how this works:

> One important result of this procedure is the great confusion it creates in the mind of every observer, friend or foe. In the end no one knows how to distinguish truth from falsehood. The totalitarian potentate, in order to break down the minds of men, first needs widespread mental chaos and verbal confusion, because both paralyze his opposition and cause the morale of the enemy to deteriorate.[14]

Inability to decipher basic fact from fiction is a defining characteristic of menticide conditioning. Under extreme duress, subjects become disoriented not just from their surroundings but also from core beliefs and even observations of the physical world around them. In this state of confusion, it becomes possible to redefine the victim's fundamental reality, undercutting resistance and opening up the possibility of reprogramming (though, as we saw in Meerloo's phase 4, Stalinism was much better at breaking minds than rebuilding them).

By no means were the Soviets alone in these mind-control tactics. The Nazis deployed very similar approaches. Dr. Meerloo had seen this firsthand as a colonel in the psychological department of the Dutch army in the UK. He interviewed many prisoners of the Nazi concentration camps who faced psychological horrors, confirming Meerloo's observation that abject confusion, to the point of delusion, is a telltale sign of menticide:

> Many victims of totalitarianism have told me in interviews that the most upsetting experience they faced in the concentration camps was the feeling of the loss of logic, the state of confusion into which they had been brought—the state in which nothing held any validity. They had arrived at the Pavlovian state of inhibition, which psychiatrists call mental disintegration or depersonalization. It seemed as if they had unlearned all their former responses and had not yet adopted new ones. But in reality they simply did not know what was what.[15]

If menticide is successful, truth and reality are distorted beyond recognition. The psychological annihilation of victims allows totalitarian captors to build something new, demanding that broken, deluded subjects begin to show gratitude for, and even celebrate, the lies they're told. This is the utmost—and final—dehumanizing goal: mental degradation.

Celebrating lies was the clearest sign that a victim was fully broken. Meerloo noted that captives of the Nazi regime could face the "crime" of "physiognomic insubordination," or merely appearing unhappy with those committing menticide against them.[16] When every fiber in their being told them to detest the pain they were receiving, they were punished for failing to appreciate their torment.

In addition to celebrating lies, victims were also required to betray their friends and families and deny their previous ethics, in essence repudiating the relationships and beliefs that made them who they used to be.

This was hauntingly depicted in the final pages of George Orwell's masterpiece, *1984*. Incarcerated for his crimes against Big Brother, Winston Smith is threatened with horrific torment: being forced to wear a mask filled with hungry rats. His only escape is to turn on his lover, Julia. Winston's relationship with Julia was the one thing that he hoped to keep sacred no matter what evil he faced. But Big Brother broke through Winston's last mental stronghold with the fear of imminent torture:

> The mask was closing on his face. The wire brushed his cheek. And then—no, it was not relief, only hope, a tiny fragment of hope. Too late, perhaps too late. But he had suddenly understood that in the whole world there was just one person to whom he could transfer his punishment— *one* body that he could thrust between himself and the rats. And he was shouting frantically, over and over. "Do it to Julia! Do it to Julia! Not me! Julia! I don't care what you do

to her. Tear her face off, strip her to the bones. Not me! Julia! Not me!"[17]

The cage door shuts as Winston betrays the only person he truly cares for. His torture is over because the destruction of his soul is complete. The totalitarianism of Big Brother has broken him beyond repair. There is no longer any chance that he will resist or defy the regime, as there is nothing for which he will fight. In the last pages of the novel, Winston sees Julia, they admit their mutual betrayal (she also denounced him under interrogation), and their bond has been erased. All that remains for Winston is his coerced, artificial love for Big Brother.

Menticide in America

Gathered around the pool, the audience was put in a strange position. Some may have freely cheered Lia Thomas's NCAA 2022 championship victory, thinking it was a win for civil rights.[18] Others may have clapped with minimal enthusiasm, hoping to avoid scrutiny for insufficiently celebrating this breakthrough moment. But every person watching that day had to know deep down—whether consciously admitting it or not—the same fundamental truth: Lia Thomas is a man.

His entire life until three years before that 500-yard women's freestyle competition, "Lia" was Will Thomas. You won't find the name Will in many of the articles written about Thomas, nor does it appear on his Wikipedia page. Any reference to the name he'd had for most of his life is forbidden as "deadnaming." Transgender transition requires the rewriting of history. And to complete the illusion, most news publications refer to Thomas with the pronoun "she" exclusively.

"I'm a woman, just like anybody else on the team," Thomas explained to *Sports Illustrated* the following year. "I've always viewed myself as just a swimmer. It's what I've done for so long; it's what I love. . . . I get into the water every day and do my best."[19]

Yet there is no more absurd manifestation of the transgender agenda than the spectacle of a biological male dominating elite women in athletic competition. In early 2023, the international body governing track and field sports decided that a man who has gone through puberty (and thus has male anatomy and musculature with a larger heart and blood oxygenation capacity) cannot compete against women in events that measure speed and strength. This was a rare (if roundabout) recent victory in the fight for sanity as a number of other athletic associations and leagues bend the knee to trans ideology.

How did National Public Radio report the track and field decision on Twitter? "The international governing body for track and field will ban trans women athletes from elite women's competitions, citing a priority for fairness over inclusion, *despite limited scientific research involving elite trans athletes* [italics mine]."[20]

Despite limited scientific research involving elite trans athletes is an astonishingly dishonest way to present this news.

In essence, NPR was saying *a man is a woman. There is no proof trans athletes have an advantage over women competitors.* But anyone who complies with this logic participates in a delusion.

We all know there is a mass delusion surrounding transgenderism. What matters to us here is *how* that mass delusion is enforced.

Today in America we're far from the gulags and show trials of Stalin's Soviet Union. But there is still overwhelming evidence that Americans are being forced to submit to a more insidious mind-killing regime as the American Left has adopted key tactics of menticide and applied them in the context of a modern techno-democracy.

The punishments for going against gender doctrine, for example, aren't beatings with broom handles and electric shock. Instead, job firings, reputational destruction, and banishment from public life are among the Left's most frequent tactics. The threats are social, not physical, but the result is still forcing people to contradict their deeply held beliefs and to disregard reality.

Take just one example: Carole Hooven, a Harvard human evolutionary biology lecturer.

In 2021, she wrote in an emailed statement to *The Harvard Crimson*, "I see that more and more educators are changing language and even backing off of controversial topics not because they think it's the right thing to do as educators, but out of fear." She went on, "This is not the right way forward. We can be caring and sensitive to the needs and identities of everyone, while also sticking to biological reality."[21]

Hooven's comments were rather banal and measured. Still, she committed an unacceptable offense, as the *Crimson* describes the response to her comments: "maintaining the existence of two sexes and defending the usage of the terms 'male' and 'female'"[22] while promoting a book she had written about testosterone on a Fox News show.

Hooven was denounced by the director of her department's diversity and inclusion task force, another department chair, and the Harvard Graduate Student Union. As a result, Hooven was unable to find any graduate students willing to work with her as teaching assistants, and she faced an intolerably hostile workplace. She was forced to take an early retirement from Harvard at age fifty-seven. While Hooven refused to sacrifice her intellectual integrity for the sake of ideological conformity, the transgender movement demonstrated its ultimate goal was to commit an act of menticide on the issue of gender and force Hooven to celebrate a lie.[23]

At the same time (and ironically) in Hooven's case the radicalized Left demonstrated their own menticide—the minds of everyone around her from Ivy League administrators to graduate students had already been killed. They freely sought to destroy a woman's life in order to deny basic biology.

Using mind-killing tactics to enforce gender bending is not limited to Ivy League campuses. A tenth grader in a Seattle public high school failed a true/false quiz by asserting it was "true" that "only men have penises and only women can get pregnant."[24]

If you were to type the question "can men menstruate" into Google's search engine, as of September 2023, the top recommended link, out of 210 million possible search results online, would be from a website called TransHub, giving the following answer:

Having a period is not a feminine thing, and people of all genders menstruate, including non-binary people, agender people, and even plenty of men! Menstruation doesn't change anything about your gender, it's just a thing that some bodies do.[25]

This is absurdly, objectively false. "People of all genders" do not menstruate—only women menstruate. And the effort to downplay the female fertility cycle to "just a thing that some bodies do" is dishonest gender-identity propaganda. As the most powerful internet search engine in the world (some would argue its most powerful corporation), Google responds to a straightforward question about human biology by promoting a source that propagates gender-identity lies.

But the escalation of the trans agenda doesn't stop here. For decades, the transgender position was that trans individuals are adults (overwhelmingly male) who wish to present as the opposite gender. Since they are legally able to consent to the medical and social consequences of such life-altering decisions as hormones and sex-change operations, the activist Left positioned it as a "live-and-let-live" issue. Why is it your business if Bob wants to be called Sally? Be polite. Adults can do with their bodies whatever they like.

But the transgender movement has expanded far beyond adults to target children. Eerily, when we analyze the "trans children" movement using the first three stages of Meerloo's framework, the Left's mind-killing agenda is clear.

Remember that Meerloo's first phase is artificial breakdown and conditioning. The media and medical establishment follow this tactic, knowingly or not, by normalizing the concept of "trans children." They employ propaganda campaigns (another tactic we'll cover in chapter 8) to convince the general public that children can be born in the wrong body. This idea, for example, has been pronounced from the White House, in official communications: "Today, in honor of Transgender Day of Visibility, the Biden-Harris Administration is uplifting transgender communities—and especially transgender kids and their families."[26]

The psychological epidemic of trans children begins with susceptible adults. In America, many Democrats target parents with moral blackmail, convincing them that they are killing children by refusing to encourage gender transition. For instance, a Biden White House government briefing from 2023 misleadingly reads, "Over half of transgender youth say they have seriously considered suicide in the last year because of the discrimination and rejection they face. In the face of these challenges, research shows that, when transgender youth are affirmed and supported, they thrive."[27] So, either support gender transitions for kids or they will die. The moral blackmail inherent in this is stunning. And the conclusion that they "thrive" is hotly debated. Over what time frame?

Meerloo's second phase is submission to and positive identification with the enemy. In the case of trans children, parents are encouraged to expose their children to trans adults. One such violation of childhood innocence is drag queen performances for kids. The Left has mounted an effort to expose children as early and often as possible to adult men dressed as women dancing in sexually provocative clothing.

This campaign received cultural support from all the usual mouthpieces on the Left. "Drag Queen Story Hour Continues Its Reign at Libraries, Despite Backlash,"[28] reads a representative piece in *The New York Times* on this issue from 2019. According to the *Times*, the problem isn't the aggressive campaign against children; it's the conservative backlash against it. Adulatory reporting from the biggest names in the mainstream media suggests that they think these performances aren't just acceptable but integral to a new civil rights struggle for trans equality. And when it's not story hours, its drag-themed shows for kids or drag queen teachers targeting minors by "covertly" placing "LGBTQ+ material" in classrooms.[29]

Why is it so important to the Left that adult men dressed as women read to children or do a striptease in front of them? Is there any benefit to education or development that comes from, say, having a forty-year-old man in a sequined cocktail dress, fishnet stockings, and six-inch heels read a storybook to toddlers? Whenever anyone has had the courage to ask these questions, the substance is ignored, and the mob howls, "Bigot!"

The adults who dance in front of the kids—and the parents who bring their own children or cheer as part of the crowd—have become accessories to a menticide. The glee is pathological, as otherwise normal parents clap and applaud while cross-dressing men encourage children to put dollar bills in their thong underwear.

Parents, once they are sufficiently confused by the dominant media and leftist narrative of gender identity, proudly subject their own children to these depraved performances. They've moved beyond blindness to embracing that which will destroy the minds of their children. Once that's done, it becomes almost impossible to convince parents that they have been pawns in a broader agenda.

Phase 3 is reconditioning to the new order—in essence a type of brainwashing we'll cover more in the next chapter. As the trans agenda expands to include children, it has taken over institutions and bureaucracies—including science and medicine. Many doctors today will tell you that, yes, "men can get pregnant," and trans kids should get "gender-affirming care." Medical professionals, parents, concerned citizens—nobody can question this "science."

Just as we saw with masking during Covid, institutional medicine has been overwhelmingly co-opted into lies once again. Here's a 2021 press release from the American Medical Association telling state legislatures that kids should be able to have the whole range of such services:

The American Medical Association (AMA) today urged governors to oppose state legislation that would prohibit medically necessary gender transition-related care for minor patients, calling such efforts "a dangerous intrusion into the practice of medicine." In a letter to the National Governors Association (NGA), the AMA cited evidence that trans and non-binary gender identities are normal variations of human identity and expression, and that forgoing gender-affirming care can have tragic health consequences, both mental and physical.[30]

There's no mention of the tragic consequences of these surgeries for many who undergo them, including much higher mortality, suicide rates, and psychiatric morbidity than the general population.[31] The only studies we can rely on involve adults; there are no long-term evaluations of what "gender-affirming care" does to children, because it hasn't been around long enough as a practice for any such studies to exist. But as with Covid's masking and vaccine mandates, the absence of evidence for "the science" of the trans agenda is too often ignored.

"Trans kids" is now a cultural movement, one with vigils, support groups, and fundraisers. It is impossible to avoid, even for apolitical parents, as schools in many jurisdictions across the country decide that boys can compete on girls' sports teams and even undress in their locker rooms and use female bathrooms. All the while, advocates gaslight concerned parents, asking, "Why are you so focused on this?" while they maniacally advance the agenda.

Children are also pressured by their peers. The concept of

rapid-onset gender dysphoria was first proposed by physician and researcher Lisa Littman, who published a paper in the journal *PLOS One* on the theory. In short, Dr. Littman found an exponential increase in the likelihood that young children will claim to be transgender if they are surrounded by peers and exposed to social media posts from those who have come out as trans.

The backlash against Dr. Littman was swift.[32] Brown University initially published a news story on her work, which was later removed, and then issued statements supporting a series of "corrections" and "addendums" that were later added to undermine its fundamental conclusion.[33] The Democrat apparatus went into a rage at the suggestion that there could be a "contagion" effect of transgender children because of their classmates or social media influences, as this would conflict with their ideological contention that children can be born "in the wrong body." Though Dr. Littman, like Hooven, didn't back down, the powerful in society were still sharpening their menticide tactics to get everyone to psychologically submit. We'll never know how many other researchers or scientists out there refused to question the regime and allowed their minds to be killed after watching what was done to others who resisted.

Those who have ever publicly defied transgender-kids orthodoxy know that they'll be met with unhinged opposition. The American Left approaches the issue with a maniacal zeal. It is now doctrine for Democrats that "women can have penises, too." Anyone with even the most rudimentary knowledge of biology must shut up or else be shouted down. All the while, delusion is forced on us by the culture, the "science," and peers. Kids, already easily influenced, have their minds reconditioned to the transgender worldview.

Now they're coming for you. In fact, to truly be considered among the elite today, you must accept the trans agenda. It's an unholy crusade: the eradication not just of gender roles but gender altogether. The totalitarian Left demands your celebration of this issue. If they can make you look at a 230-pound, bearded, middle-aged man who has suddenly changed his name and wears dresses, and you proclaim on cue, "That's a woman!", they've successfully killed your mind.

You are now a party to their lie, a victim of menticide.

Children, I've found, are often unfortunate victims of mental contagions—and not only in the United States. A 2007 headline in *Newsweek* reads "Iraqi Prison Tries to Un-Brainwash Radical Youth."[34] The article details how Camp Cropper, near Baghdad, was bursting with 3,800 detainees— 747 of them minors.[35] Many of them had been initially threatened by the insurgents. But those who fully radicalized were not only willing to join terrorist groups like AQI. They would seek martyrdom through suicide bombings. They were willing to kill themselves and others, including women and children.

What we saw at Camp Cropper was beyond menticide. These kids didn't just accept the worldview of their psychologically abusive masters. They didn't have their old ideas erased and simply replaced. They embraced the new ideas with a fanatical zeal. They became willing to die—and even kill—for them.

There was a term—brainwashing—that frequently came up in discussions of these kids.

But where did this term come from? And what is brainwashing?

That story begins in Maoist China—though the Maoist regime called it "thought reform." After victims had their minds killed, they were "reeducated" to believe complicated Marxist theories. Some of them renounced their most deeply held beliefs, donning the new ideology of their tormentors long after they were freed from the most intense measures of Communist compulsion.

During my time in Mosul, "brainwashed" suicide bombers were a major focus of US military and CIA operations. Many were coming from other countries and overseas—so-called foreign fighters.

To find out exactly how this murderous pipeline worked, I traveled to the Iraq–Syria border to connect with Special Forces teams and learn more about the brainwashing that was behind all the mayhem.

3

Brainwashing

Iraq–Syria Border, 2007

For the first time in Iraq, I'd been told C-4 and dusty ATVs were our fallback. The Green Berets called it their "Alamo Plan."

They were giving me a tour of the sandbagged warehouse they called home. The roof was rigged with plastic explosives. In case they were overrun, explosions on time delay would bring the whole thing crashing down.

The handful of nearby ATVs were parked under a rusty shed and ready to go facing the open Iraqi desert. It was a heck of an exit plan. But I knew from military reporting I'd read back at Langley that they'd had a suicide car bomber detonate at their front gate a few months before. In this part of Iraq—far from major reinforcements—their extreme preparations made sense.

It was 2007, the height of the Sunni Iraqi insurgency. CIA higher-ups had sent me out to this (godforsaken) part of the world—a land port right on the Iraq–Syria border—to collect intelligence from forward-deployed troops and whatever sources they had in the area. Standing on the roof of a US Special Forces team outpost, I observed hundreds of trucks and cars snaking their way through poorly manned checkpoints. Almost none were searched, and some were certain to be carrying contraband, including weapons, suicide vests, and would-be martyrs for the ongoing jihad.

Just one year prior, AQI bombed the golden mosque in Samarra. Since that attack, suicide bombings had become the most devastating tactic of the jihadists. Scores of civilians would be killed at once in a single blast, with hundreds of additional casualties from shrapnel. AQI targets were most often Iraqi security forces and civilians, not coalition troops. Their plan was to force Iraq into all-out sectarian war. This would allow AQI to unite all the Sunni Muslim militants, seize power across the country, and expel the US and allied forces.

After gathering the intel I needed in source meetings, my team and I left the port and hitched a helicopter ride to an even more remote Special Forces outpost in the Sinjar region. This was essentially a house in the desert surrounded by barbed wire and concrete vehicle barriers. The Special Forces soldiers there were deeply knowledgeable about the suicide bomber networks in the province.

These guys were door-kickers straight out of a Tom Clancy novel, and we got along well. They asked me if I'd travel with them in thin-skinned (unarmored) pickup trucks to a meeting the next day to dive deeper into the jihadist facilitation networks. I was game, but my bosses ordered me to come back for a debrief.

That same Special Forces team took down a suspected suicide bomber–facilitator on a road the day I flew out of Sinjar. When they approached the high-value target with M4s drawn, the target clacked off a suicide vest, and ball bearings hit several of the team (thankfully, none of the Americans were killed, and all made full recoveries).

Suicide bombers were the most devastating, terrifying weapon of the Iraq War from 2003 to 2008. IEDs (improvised explosive devices) caused the most overall casualties, but it was suicide bombers who created the most terror in the civilian population. The Sunni insurgency was able to produce an army of suicide bombers. They would use vehicles laden with explosives, sometimes hundreds of pounds of them. With that kind of explosive payload, a bomber could level entire buildings in one blast and kill hundreds. And for even more up-close mayhem, AQI unleashed suicide vest wearers, usually to infiltrate markets and densely packed civilian locations. There was a seemingly end-less stream of these suicide-murder bombers.

But how? What could possibly drive otherwise normal Muslim men to travel around the world (in the case of "foreign fight-ers") to willingly kill themselves and murder dozens of innocent people?

Suicidal militancy is not a new weapon of warfare. The word *assassin* comes from a medieval Shi'ite Islamic sect, the Nizari Isma'ili, who were trained to kill specific targets on command, often with a dagger, usually at the expense of their own lives. They were the original terror sleeper cells, willing to bide their time, deeply infiltrate the environment of their target, then strike, knowing there would be no escape for them. Leg-end has it that these original assassins took drugs—hashish—to achieve a state of euphoria and to suppress all fear. From that alleged practice of using hashish ("hashishi") we get, over time, the word *assassin*—though historians still argue over the exact derivation.[1]

More recently, the Japanese deployed suicidal militants in World War II as kamikazes. Meaning "divine wind" in Japa-nese (a reference to a typhoon that, in AD 1281, wrecked a Mongol invasion fleet),[2] kamikaze pilots intentionally flew their planes, laden with explosives, into the hulls of American ships in the Pacific theater. Beginning with the Battle of Leyte Gulf in October 1944, thousands of these suicide bomber pilots were used to halt the Allied advance. While devastating in battle, the tactic didn't prevail in the end—the Japanese lost the war anyway.

What kind of psychological manipulation compels suicidal militancy? The CIA had given its counterterrorism analysts, like me, extensive training in this ideological cycle, drawn from decades of Agency expertise.

Here's what I learned: Creating a suicide bomber first requires destroying any beliefs that would prevent a person from killing himself and others. Often, bad actors manipulate a subject's extreme feelings of guilt or hopelessness, playing on their fears.

But it was in the aftermath of World War II, in the early days of the Cold War, that a new term to describe this systematic mind wiping and reeducation would emerge:

Brainwashing.

From POW to Communist

The American journalist Edward Hunter was the first to use the term *brainwashing* in his 1950 *Miami Daily News* article "Brain-Washing Tactics Force Chinese Into Ranks Of Communist Party." The word itself was Hunter's direct translation of the Mandarin for *xi* ("wash") and *nao* ("brain"). In his article, Hunter described how Mao Tse-tung's Red Army used brutal, ancient Chinese tactics to hypnotize citizens. Hunter warned that the goal of brainwashing was to wipe the mind of all previously held beliefs and replace them with new ideology, turning the citizen into a puppet of the government.

Hunter was formerly an information operations agent of the Office of Strategic Services (the precursor to the CIA) during World War II.[3] As a former intelligence officer, he learned psychological warfare, which is necessary even if you're fighting for the good guys. While reporting on Communist China, Hunter learned about Maoist mind-control practices and believed brainwashing "described a strategy that had yet no name."[4]

Many critics and experts in psychology dismiss Hunter's work on brainwashing, often citing his lack of medical or scientific credentials. However, as a fellow former intelligence officer, I know information warfare is best understood not by academics but by practitioners.

The truth is, Hunter was onto something, if only by describing a phenomenon that had not yet been defined. The totalitarian regimes of the twentieth century proved you could emotionally and psychologically cripple a person with intense, focused effort and then build them back up to believe self-contradictory political theories—even mass delusions. Much like menticide, some of the victims of this process would develop ideological attachment and even fondness for their mental torturers that would last long after their official captivity and reeducation. Yet brainwashing went further. If menticide was designed to break people like Winston and Julia in *1984*, brainwashing was supposed to create people like Sergeant Raymond Shaw in *The Manchurian Candidate*, totally subservient to their masters and willing to further their goals.

Perhaps Hunter's most important discovery was not about how regimes broke people down but about the immense pressure and repetition used to build a new person. This final stage of brainwashing—which the Chinese called "reeducation"— was used in real life, during wartime, and on a massive scale, to turn people's minds against what they had previously held dear. Mao's tyrannical regime would do this to hundreds of millions of Chinese.

But can it happen here? Is it possible to brainwash Americans, whose national identity is rooted in skepticism of authority, especially the government? History proves that the answer is yes. To see how, we can look to the Korean War, when Maoists captured and brainwashed American prisoners.

Their betrayal of military oaths, abandonment of Americanism, and full submission to a Communist delusion would shock the world.

It started in May 1952, when two American airmen captured by North Korea, First Lieutenants John Quinn and Kenneth Enoch, were quoted in Communist news outlets confessing their use of bioweapons against China and Korea. According to their statements, the "warmongers of Wall Street"[5] had pushed for a campaign of germ warfare against Chinese and North Korean forces. These two American servicemen were the first, but dozens of other captured airmen would follow with similar confessions.

During the Korean War, the North Korean Communists alleged in official public statements that the United States had deployed biological weapons against them. Initially they claimed American forces had spread smallpox in North Korea.[6] The following year they alleged that US forces had dropped insects from planes to spread plague, cholera, and other lethal pathogens.

Internal documents obtained after the Soviet Union's collapse proved that the bioweapons propaganda campaign was false. It was fabricated with help from the Soviet Union to undermine US credibility on the world stage.[7] Still, the allegations sparked an international outcry and heated debates at the United Nations, under whose auspices the Korean War was taking place.

As with most propaganda campaigns, there was a grain of truth to the allegations about bio-weapons war crimes. At the time of the war, diseases like plague, meningitis, and cholera were still endemic in North Korea—and public fears of these ailments loomed large. The war itself raised the likelihood of outbreaks. Additionally, at the end of World War II, American forces had seized an experimental facility for biological weapons, Imperial Japan's infamous Unit 731, and had begun using the lab to create vaccines and antidotes against biological or chemical weapons.

The Communist alliance of Soviet Union, China, and North Korea knew of this effort, and twisted it for shock value.

Still, the allegations that America was conducting biological warfare were just that—enemy allegations—until the Communists rolled out their brainwashed secret weapons, dubbed "the turncoats."

Both North Korean and US forces had taken large numbers of POWs off the battlefield, and many of the Communist forces did not want to return home. Approximately fifty thousand enemy North Korean and Chinese soldiers decided to stay in the West after the war.[8] At the time of the armistice signing in July 1953, only twenty-three Americans would abandon their home country and stay in North Korea. These men became known as the turncoats. They were a propaganda coup for the Communists, and their conversion was years in the making.

North Korea systematically exploited these Americans—as well as all their captives—as part of an unprecedented psychological warfare campaign. These men were subjected to extreme tactics of coercion and prisoner deprivation while in custody, including isolation, malnutrition, and sleep deprivation. Unsurprisingly, the death rate of Americans held in POW camps in

Korea and China were similar (38 percent)[9] to what Americans had suffered under the notoriously inhumane Japanese in World War II (40 percent).[10]

Around 5,000 of the estimated 7,200 US POWs signed petitions to end the war,[11] and many confessed to heinous, false crimes. But the real shock came in the fall of 1953, when a group of American prisoners appeared on Communist radio and television. They wore the clothing of the Chinese military, stood in front of Chinese news crews, and spoke about their fear of returning to America for their positions against racism and capitalism. Like thousands of other American POWs, they also signed peace petitions. But these men—the turncoats— were active participants in the defamation of their country, and they said they no longer wished to return to America. During one of the televised propaganda sessions, when a Chinese voice off camera asked the turncoats whether they wanted to go home, the POWs shouted "No!" in unison.[12]

It was shocking that anyone would want to remain in the hell that was Maoist China. And many of them clung to that decision to the end. But some of the twenty-three turncoats did decide to return to America after experiencing the reality of Communism in China for themselves. Initially they were welcomed. Then, the US military decided that they had committed treason, giving aid and comfort to the enemy. They were court-martialed and handed down harsh prison sentences of ten to twenty years each.

Despite the risks of prosecution, more POW airmen returned home to the US. By then, the US military realized these weren't normal cases of traitors. These POWs had been psychologically broken and exploited in a systematic fashion. In a written statement collected by USAF Psychological Warfare Division, the airmen said they'd been programmed into becoming "living dead men, controlled human robots" following the Communists' commands.[13]

This brainwashing of American POWs in the Korean War captured the attention of the freethinking world. These captured Americans weren't just saying they were opposed to the war; they were lying about US war crimes, spewing absurd Communist rhetoric, and apparently believing it all.

How did the Communists go about this wiping and rewiring of American soldiers' brains? They used the same systematic, sophisticated brainwashing techniques that the Communists had used against the Chinese population and foreigners inside China considered "subversives" or "counterrevolutionaries."

To understand how the Communists were trying to achieve mind control over a massive population (then estimated to be nearly six hundred million), an American psychiatrist named Robert Jay Lifton traveled to Hong Kong in 1954, where he met with twenty-five Westerners and fifteen Chinese subjects who had been put through Maoist thought reform programs.

There Lifton discovered a machinery of mind control that, if followed with enough conviction, could break and remake minds in any culture in any time.

Including our own.

Mao's Brainwashing Playbook: Thought Reform

Brainwashing—or "thought reform," as it was officially called—was the central ideological effort of the Communist project in Maoist China. Robert Jay Lifton believed it was "one of the most powerful efforts at human manipulation ever undertaken."[14] While Lifton acknowledged that all regimes throughout history have imposed an ideology on their people, he thought "the Chinese communists have brought to theirs a more organized, comprehensive . . . a more *total* character . . . as well as a unique blend of energetic and ingenious psychological techniques."[15]

In 1942, Mao gave a speech justifying the party's brainwashing campaign. He said that he was doing society a favor by eradicating anti-Communists:

Two principles must be observed. The first is, "punish the past to warn the future," and the second, "save men by curing their ills." Past errors must be exposed with no thought of personal feelings or face. We must use a scientific attitude to analyze and criticize what has been undesirable in the past . . . this is the meaning of "punish the past to warn the future." But our object in exposing errors and criticizing shortcomings is like that of a doctor in curing a disease. . . . [We must have] an attitude of saving men by curing their diseases.[16]

Mao framed anti-Communism as a virus or dangerous bacteria that must be eliminated. His Chinese Communist Party officially used the terms *szu-hsiang kai-tsao* (translated as "ideological molding" or "ideological reform") to describe this eradication process.

The West understood what Mao was trying to do, but it was Lifton who uncovered how it worked. Over the course of seventeen months in Hong Kong, Lifton's psychiatric research became the basis for a seminal book on brainwashing titled *Thought Reform and the Psychology of Totalism*, in which he documented the systematized, relentless procedures of Maoist brainwashing. Lifton came to believe "the combination of *external force or coercion* with an appeal to *inner enthusiasm through evangelistic exhortation* . . . gave thought reform its emotional scope and power."[17]

It wasn't enough to break the minds of captives—a process

the Soviets had already mastered by the time Mao seized control of the Chinese mainland. Prisoners had to be turned into unquestioning supporters of the Communist ideology used to break them. From his in-depth interviews with victims, Lifton identified two phases—confession and reeducation—that formed the framework for every case of brainwashing. Lifton writes, "thought reform consists of two basic elements: *confession*, the exposure and renunciation of past and present 'evil'; and *reeducation*, the remaking of a man in the Communist image."[18] Through the two phases of confession and reeducation, it's possible to analyze brainwashing transformation.

In essence, brainwashing is built on wiping away the old man and replacing him with the new. Ultimately, all mind-control tactics are focused on one or both of those goals. For people to be controlled, they must be separated from their former self. For people to be remade, they must have a new self imposed upon them.

That's what Lifton found in his groundbreaking research. One of his notable interviewees was Dr. Charles Vincent, a foreign physician in Shanghai who had been imprisoned in China for more than three years when Mao seized power. Like so many other foreigners in China at the time of the Communist takeover, Dr. Vincent was imprisoned on suspicion of espionage charges. These charges were patently absurd—no evidence was presented against him, and he was afforded no due-process rights of any kind. But the brainwashing he suffered is still considered one of the preeminent case studies in the field.

Thought Reform Phase I: Confession

In the case of Dr. Vincent, his confession required a sustained "assault upon identity," beginning with his arrest.[19] His captors immediately demanded that Vincent confess to crimes he had not committed. Any objection to the accusations resulted in more severe punishment. This caused Dr. Vincent to wonder whether he had done something wrong.

Following the initial calls for confession, captors then establish feelings of guilt in subjects through endless interrogations and accusations. The subject is also deprived of sleep and food and is often beaten during this period. Like menticide, the psychic stresses are combined with psychological duress—all supposedly because of the subject's transgressions. The brainwashers insist all the pain and confusion of the subject are his own fault.

The next step is the "self-betrayal," where the abused and demoralized subjects begin to concoct stories in order to make the punishment stop. The interrogators do not accept these stories of guilt, no matter how severe, and demand greater "sincerity."

As Lifton recounted from Dr. Vincent's ordeal, "he was constantly told by his cellmates that he was completely responsible for his own plight. ('You want the chains! You want to be shot! . . . Otherwise you would be more "sincere" and the chains would not be necessary.') . . . he could neither understand exactly what he was guilty of ('recognize his crimes') nor could he in any way establish his innocence."[20] Every impulse Dr. Vincent had to try to reclaim some shred of sanity was undermined with a remorseless barrage of Communist slogans.

Eventually, the subject reaches "the breaking point," according to Dr. Lifton, when:

You are annihilated . . . exhausted . . . you can't control yourself, or remember what you said two minutes before. You feel that all is lost. . . . From that moment, the judge is the real master of you. You accept anything he says. When he asks how many "intelligences" you gave to that person, you just put out a number in order to satisfy him. If he says, "Only those?" you say, "No, there are more." If he says, "One hundred," you say, "One hundred". . . . You do whatever they want. You don't pay any more attention to your life or to your handcuffed arms. You can't distinguish right from left. You just wonder when you will be shot—and begin to hope for the end of all this.[21]

In this first stage of brainwashing, Dr Vincent's captors were committing menticide against him. Like so many other victims, he was forced to abandon his attachment to the truth. He eagerly confessed guilt for things he had not done and began to believe he must have done something—anything—to bring this relentless psychological torture on himself. Vincent even began to believe his jailers' refrain that he must have done something wrong, because as they constantly told him, the Party does not make mistakes. He was made to write and rewrite his confession, over and over. It was never "sincere" enough.

At this moment of absolute hopelessness the prisoner is primed for reality to be rewritten. Their captive's mind is as close as possible to a blank slate. Welcome to phase 2.

Thought Reform Phase 2: Reeducation

Now the ideological training begins. This is what most people colloquially refer to as brainwashing—the positive construction of a new ideology after someone's mind has been wiped clean. The subject is encouraged to see things from the "people's standpoint," which means reframing all their actions through Communist dogma. But as this begins, the handcuffs come off and chains are removed. Better food and overall holding conditions are given to the subject—so long as the "progress" toward the people's standpoint continues. Both the body and mind become conditioned to recognize the "people's standpoint" as a positive.

In this phase, Dr. Vincent's brainwashers began to treat him with some dignity, and even occasional kindness. His cellmates (who were Communist plants) would go through Maoist orthodoxy with him in detail. Dr. Vincent told Lifton that "by adopting the 'people's standpoint,' he channels nonspecific feelings of guilt into a paranoid, pseudo-logical system. His sense of evil, formerly vague and free-floating, is now made to do specific work for reform."[22]

As he continues, the reeducation escalates. Dr. Vincent's captors force him into a group study program (*hsüeh hsi* in Chinese) for up to sixteen hours a day.[23] Dr. Vincent described the reeducation class almost like a Western college seminar—inmates were referred to as "schoolmates" and prison officials were "instructors"—except only the most rigid Communist dogma was allowed:

Led by the cell chief, its procedure was simple enough: one prisoner read material from a Communist newspaper, book, or pamphlet; and then each in turn was expected to express his own opinion and to criticize the views of others. Everyone was required to participate actively, and anyone who did not was severely criticized. Each had to learn to express himself from the "correct" or "people's standpoint"—applied not only to personal actions but to political, social, and ethical issues. With each of the prisoners feeling that his freedom

or even his life might be at stake, the zeal of the participants was overwhelming.[24]

In time, the indoctrination becomes so complete that the
subject believes the orthodoxy. In Dr. Vincent's case, he began
seeing all things through the lens of "the people's standpoint,"
and fully embraced his new life as a "progressive." He also developed a distrust bordering on contempt for the Western, capitalist
world from which he came. With his mind fully reeducated and
his spirit broken, the Maoist torturers expelled Dr. Vincent
from the country.

The freedom he was afforded in Hong Kong did not immediately bring Dr. Vincent back to his old self. In fact, the Chinese Communist thought reform process had been so effective,
he told Lifton, "It is not that I miss it, but I find that it was
more easy."[25] He was even initially hostile toward the West and
defensive of some aspects of Communist ideology for months
after his release.

Over time, Dr. Vincent would slowly recognize the trauma
he had been put through for what it truly was: brainwashing.
He developed contempt for his captors but remained shaky in
his sense of himself, and of his future. Brainwashing had a lasting effect on Dr. Vincent, though on a hopeful note, it fell short
of its ultimate goal of total, lasting mind control.

The Maoist brainwashing process, first identified as such by

Edward Hunter and studied in detail by Lifton, was a policy applied across the entire sweep of China. It would grow to reach its pinnacle with the Cultural Revolution. This was the top-to-bottom, society-wide program to indoctrinate every citizen in Marxist theory in the 1960s and 1970s. Every aspect of Chinese life, from schoolchildren entering the classroom to senior party meetings, had to be soaked in official dogma. Brainwashing in China was imposed through the inescapable voice in every ear demanding obedience on every possible matter of life, from the most major to the most minute, all backed by the threat of torture, imprisonment, and death for non-compliance.

Chinese reeducation ranks among the darkest chapters of psychological warfare in the twentieth century. By cowing the population into obedience, it directly enabled Mao's Great Leap Forward, from 1958 to 1962, which in turn caused China's Great Famine, from 1959 to 1961.

It was the most lethal famine in history, with estimates of the death toll varying from eighteen million to forty-two million people[26]—and brainwashing was the genesis of it all.

Cults of Personality

Lifton's two-phase playbook, while illuminating, doesn't describe every facet of mind control. Lifton wrote—and history showed—that in addition to confession and reeducation, there's very often something else behind every brainwashing agenda: a powerful, charismatic engineer.

This is especially true when brainwashing large groups. How, for instance, did Shoko Asahara—who masterminded the Aum Shinrikyō cult's sarin nerve gas attack on the Tokyo subway in 1995—attract more than ten thousand cult members throughout Japan and Russia? Lifton answers this question in his discussion of demagogues in his book *Destroying the World to Save It*.

Shoko Asahara became, according to Lifton, "a spiritual teacher whose insight is based on personal revelation, often taking the form of a vision understood to come directly from a deity."[27] Asahara adopted the "narrative of the guru—of the religious founder in general—[which] can be seen as a version of the myth of the hero."[28] Once he had constructed this foundational narrative, Asahara went to work convincing his followers that he was also a "genius in virtually every field of human endeavor."[29] And ultimately, his followers came to believe that he was the "first 'enlightened one' since Buddha."[30]

Like many of today's jihadist converts, many of Asahara's followers were intelligent, functional members of society—including Japanese science and engineering students—before they were brainwashed. Yet Asahara was able to convince them that he was a prophet and that the US would use nuclear weapons against Japan. His followers took him so seriously that twenty-four of them ran for Japan's House of Representatives (and lost).

Asahara's end goal was to hasten the end of the world through nuclear war. His followers actively sought nuclear weapons and hoped to bring about a global nuclear holocaust—they believed they would be the only ones to survive it. The cult also had a fully operational biological weapons research program with the goal of causing a worldwide pandemic, killing hundreds of millions. But members even traveled to Africa during an Ebola outbreak to capture and weaponize that highly contagious, lethal hemorrhagic fever. Fortunately for the world, these efforts failed.

While it fell short of igniting a global pandemic, the cult still racked up a grim body count. In 1989, Asahara's followers murdered a family in their sleep because the father was a lawyer working on a class-action suit against the cult. A year before their sarin nerve gas attack in the Tokyo metro, they intentionally released sarin in a residential neighborhood—causing seven deaths and five hundred hospitalizations.

Were these cult members all insane psychopaths, or victims brainwashed into a delusion? It's difficult to say. After Asahara was imprisoned, a court-appointed psychiatrist determined he was mentally competent to stand trial. Asahara's followers, according to Dr. Lifton, were willing to pay $1,000 for a liter of his bathwater (because of its magic properties) and $10,000 for a vial of his blood, which they would drink.[31]

Any expert will tell you that—generally speaking—cult members don't necessarily become vulnerable to brainwashing because they're ignorant or economically desperate. Instead, they have deeper psychological weaknesses—private insecurities— that a demagogue skillfully targets and manipulates.

Like so many cult victims, Shoko Asahara's followers were searching for greater purpose and answers to existential questions, and Asahara—having studied Buddhism and Hinduism and traveled to India to meet the Dalai Lama—seemed positioned to give it to them. His followers were wealthy young adults from influential families[32] whose elevated status in society made recruitment of other members easier.

Unsurprisingly, Asahara mandated that his followers donate their money to his cult. Asahara used those millions to live a lavish lifestyle that he didn't even try to hide—he rode around in a white Rolls-Royce. As for his followers, for giving away all their worldly possessions and their psychological freedom, they gained psychological nirvana.

As Dr. Lifton describes it, "at the heart of charisma is the leader's ability to instill and sustain feelings of vitality and immortality, feelings that reach into the core of each disciple's often wounded, always questioning self, while propelling that self beyond itself. Such feelings can be as fragile as they are psychologically explosive."[33]

This yearning for vitality and immortality is what demagogues exploit to brainwash their followers. They want their disciples to feel deeply insecure about themselves and lost in the world around them. They then convince members that they've been found, belong, and are special now. Everything will be amazing going forward, but only because of their guru and his shared revelations.

A demagogue cannot risk his followers feeling secure and emotionally stable, because people with those traits have the context to question their leader and the self-esteem to stand up for themselves when abused or manipulated. That's why cult leaders weaponize shame and force confessions—just as with Maoist reeducation. Dr. Lifton writes that "disciples, even the highest ones, engaged in a perpetual, Sisyphean struggle for purity, their guilt and shame mechanisms taken over by the cult if not by the guru himself. An ethos of confession can provide a continuing mechanism for negative self-evaluation."[34]

The demagogue convinces followers they aren't just entering a much better world by following him; they're leaving behind the unclean, worthless version of themselves they quietly loathed. All they thought they knew—and the relationships that held meaning for them (including family)—are to be abandoned forever. A disciple's questions or misgivings are dismissed as remnants of their previous life, and everything about their former selves is explicitly condemned as impure.

Under the influence of a demagogue, even one's vocabulary changes—whether the demagogue controls an end-of-days cult like Aum Shinrikyō or a Communist apparatus in a totalitarian state like the former Soviet Union or North Korea today. Only words that affirm the mandated orthodoxy are permitted. The demagogue pays particular attention to word choice, because then every time followers communicate, they're reinforcing their submission.

The "loading of the language," as described by Dr. Lifton, is a tactic common to all demagogues. In policing followers' speech, "words become limited to those that affirm the prevailing ideological claims. . . . At the same time a principle of doctrine over person requires all private perceptions to be subordinated to those ideological claims. . . . [Any doubts] were attributed to a disciple's residual defilement."[35] Of course we see this around us today when progressive demagogues demand we replace "breastfeeding" with "chestfeeding" and "illegal alien" with "migrant." The demand for preferred pronouns and ideological jargon is a demand for submission.

The mind control guru wants to come as close as possible to subjugating the souls of adherents. As long as the guru is the sole arbiter of dedication to the cult's beliefs, there's always a way for him to squeeze more obedience out of his followers.

Nothing is ever good enough. Nobody is ever devoted enough. No one is ever sincere enough.

Stalin: A Cult Leader on a World-Historic Scale

The parallels between a cult leader like Asahara and a dictator like Stalin are remarkable. Despite asking everything of their people and giving nothing tangible in return, both Asahara and Stalin commanded the total obedience of their follows, many of whom worshiped them with genuine zeal. They are different, however, in that Asahara had ten thousand followers and Stalin had tens of millions.

Despite his adopted nom de guerre (Stalin means "man of steel"), he was no warrior, nor was he a great scholar or orator. He started out life as Josip "Soso" Dzughashvili in the poor republic of Georgia, on the fringe of the collapsing Russian Empire.[36] The man who would become Stalin was a bank robber and Communist pamphleteer early on but ended his life with vast domains under his control and thousands of nuclear missiles at his disposal.

How did this happen?

Certainly, a confluence of unique historical factors favored young Soso (Stalin); for example, even before he was born, the Romanov dynasty was crumbling. But he was also a voracious reader who weaponized his knowledge with sophisticated arguments—which compensated for his lack of personal charisma. His persona as the model Soviet man—virile, enlightened, and thriving, thanks to Communism—was carefully crafted.

Ultimately, Stalin was able to build and deploy a vast machine to brainwash his citizens, from intensive propaganda campaigns to show trials to the perennial threat of the gulag. This even led to the creation of, as Anita Pisch described it, the "Stalin prize . . . conceived in 1939 to coincide with Stalin's 60th birthday . . . as a Soviet equivalent to the Nobel Prize. . . . Artistic works that contributed to the genre of the leader cult enjoyed a 'privileged' status in the competition."[37]

Stalin provided a blueprint on demagoguery for tyrants who came after him. Mao Tse-tung, Pol Pot, and the Kim dynasty of North Korea all borrowed heavily from Stalinist tactics, including the iconography of the leader as demigod. This is why Stalinist states for the past hundred years have been covered in statues, posters, and constant media and artistic hagiography of "the dear leader" in one form or another.

While Stalin used the state to elevate himself to godlike status in the Soviet Union, he understood mass psychology well enough to retain at least the pretense of modesty. As Pisch wrote, "Stalin had to appear as if he was actively discouraging the excesses of adulation directed at him, which was always to seem as if coming from below."[38] (The supreme Soviet commander didn't want all that power; the people simply insisted!)

Of course, Stalin's image as merely a comrade thrust into his position by universal acclaim was one of history's great lies. In actuality, he meticulously managed his public image from behind closed doors (and ordered the execution of anyone who questioned his power or—he believed—lacked total loyalty).

All this worked as a form of brainwashing. Stalin is in power only because the people want him there. Why? Because everyone says so. Nobody can—or even wants to—contradict Stalin's authority. Why? Because those who do disappear. Social and physical pressure is applied over an elongated period of time, the only language used is approved by the cult leader, and eventually people lose any reference to reality. The only way they can view the world is through the lens of the cult erected around them.

The result: The tyrannical demagogue creates a society that resembles a giant insane asylum. Mental illness becomes a mandatory condition to survive. Delusion is required. Meerloo even offers the diagnosis that "the totalitarian mind is like the schizophrenic mind; it has a contempt for reality."[39] And even those who maintain some dignity and keep the truth in their minds are, through the boot heels of the state, forced into a constant heightened anxiety and depression. Everyone is forced—essentially at gunpoint—to mouth the debasing slogans and lies of the regime. As Meerloo described it, people enter a demoralized, loveless abyss:

> In Totalitaria, there is no faith in fellow men, no *caritas*, no love, because real relationships between men do not exist, just as they do not exist between schizophrenics. There is only faith in and subjection to the feeding system, a fear of being totally lost, comparable with the schizophrenic's feeling of rejection and fear of reality. In the midst of spiritual loneliness and isolation, there is the fear of still greater loneliness, of more painful isolation.[40]

Unlike the new religious movement cult leader who flatters, manipulates, and schemes with limited power—the demagoguery of a tyrant like Stalin is at its core rooted in unlimited power. Whether the people believe the official lies or not is beside the point, because they have to live as though they are true. And that itself contributes to brainwashing.

When the truth has been abused so much, the masses either cannot discern fact from fiction or no longer think it makes a difference to do so. They silently suffer the indignity of walking past statues of their tormentors and read headlines on the front page of the state-owned newspapers that aren't just untrue— they do violence to the concept of truth. Slowly but surely, reality becomes what Stalin, and the state, say it is. And the impacts of this mass brainwashing can still be felt today.

In 2021, a Moscow-based pollster found that despite the brutality of his regime and the sixty million deaths attributed to it by some estimates, "70 percent of Russians approve of Stalin and his policies."[41] This is undoubtedly in part a result of Russian president Vladimir Putin's campaign to rehabilitate the tyrant legitimately credited with the Soviet Union's victory over Nazi Germany in World War II. But such a large degree of support would be impossible if the elder generation that lived under Communism had not been trained, in at least some small way, to love the man who first built the regime that had imprisoned them.

Brainwashing isn't always successful. But, as Meerloo writes in *The Rape of the Mind*, "In a country like ours, where it is up to the voting public to discern the truth, a universal knowledge of the methods used by the demagogue to deceive or to lull the public is absolutely necessary."[42]

That is why, like in every society where it's been tried, brainwashing in America requires the proliferation of falsehoods throughout society. Thankfully, we don't have gulags and firing squads, but there are other, more subtle means to brainwash Americans and push them into mass delusion.

America's Cultural Revolution

More than twenty years ago I witnessed the early stages of brainwashing firsthand—not among the jihadists in Iraq or in Communist China, but rather at my alma mater, Amherst College, during resident counselor training. We were student-employees of the college, picked by fellow students in a competitive selection process to offer housing resources and schedule educational events. A "diversity educator" was brought in to explain to us what was meant by "educational events."

First, we were told to stand on one side of the room if we were heterosexual. Then we were told to further separate based on whether our parents could afford tuition to the school, if we had ever felt the sting of discrimination, if we would consider ourselves "privileged"—and at the end, straight white male athletes were all standing alone on one side of the room. We were meant to feel ashamed of this.

And then the next phase began: telling us how to become "allies" and what we could do to make up for our evil white male hetero ways. Being forced to stand to the side was our implied confession. Embracing allyship was the beginning of our reeducation. The only thing we were missing was a cult leader.

But the college ideologues at Amherst weren't just using an

approach strikingly similar to Lifton's two-phase brainwashing process to induce hysteria in its students. They were also imposing another form of manipulation common to tyrants called collective guilt.

Yet again, Mao Tse-tung and the Communists were masters in this arena. They created a narrative of collective guilt so that individuals were responsible not just for what they did, but for what others in their group had done. Not only did this force people individually to feel the need to confess imagined sins and thus begin the brainwashing process, it also freed the mob to engage in violence against people who had done nothing wrong—because they were part of a group or held an idea deemed wrong. Communist Chinese prison regulations, quoted by Lifton in *Thought Reform and the Psychology of Totalism*, made this tactic explicit—certain thoughts weren't just wrong, they were *illegal, and the people who had them were inherently criminals*:

> In dealing with the criminals . . . [we must] educate them in the admission of guilt and obedience to the law, political and current events, labor production, and culture, so as to expose the nature of the crime committed, thoroughly *wipe out criminal thoughts, and establish a new moral code* [emphasis mine].[43]

Today this guilt-inducing approach is applied all across American politics, especially the diversity, equity, and inclusion (DEI) industry. I can't help but wonder if the Maoist party members of seventy years ago would recognize many of their tactics today.

After all, one can easily observe the steps that Lifton identified playing out. First, with its emphasis on coercing confessions. It's easy to recall examples. For instance, in recent years, a slew of government bodies across the country decided to open their official business—at every meeting, in perpetuity—with a "land acknowledgment" statement. When Sacramento, California's City Council voted to begin all meetings in this way, they offered up the following text as mandatory preamble for all official business:

Please rise for the opening acknowledgements in honor of Sacramento's Indigenous People and Tribal Lands.

To the original people of this land.

The Nisenan people, the Southern Maidu, Valley and Plains Miwok, Patwin Wintun peoples, and the people of the Wilton Rancheria, Sacramento's only Federally recognized Tribe.

May we acknowledge and honor the Native people who came before us and still walk beside us today on these ancestral lands by choosing to gather together today in the active practice of acknowledgement and appreciation for Sacramento's Indigenous People's history, contributions, and lives.

Thank you.[44]

These "land acknowledgments" are a public confession of collective guilt in the "extermination of native peoples" meant to implicate every non-Native American. It doesn't matter that nobody alive today was involved in the conquest of "native" land. We are all guilty. And these government bodies are confessing on our behalf so that they can advocate for government action on our behalf as well, usually in the form of reparations.

An even more stark example of compelled confession came after the George Floyd riots in May and June 2020. Many people in law enforcement felt compelled to kneel in solidarity with racial justice protestors—seeing it from the "people's standpoint," as Dr. Vincent's captors might have put it. Officers in Coral Gables, Florida, took the knee despite some of the protesters shouting "no justice, no peace, no racist police" at them while they were making their gesture of submission.[45] A portrait of degradation, and a public proclamation of confession from the cops, buttressed the lie that law enforcement is systemically racist.

I could fill this book with examples from the last five years. Almost everyone who works and lives in America has, by now, been forced to participate in, or at least witness, a shame-provoking DEI ritual designed as a form of brainwashing.

Of course, it doesn't stop with forced confession. The DEI industry is quick to provide reeducation as well.

A series of publicly available documents from the University of South Florida, for example—highlighted by journalist Christopher Rufo—exposes the step-by-step reeducation processes the DEI industry enacts. Rufo writes that, after forcing students to admit to their white privilege, these training documents tell them to work on "white identity development" through counseling sessions that are divided by race.[46] In addition, the white students are intended to "enter a phase of 'reintegration,' thinking, 'it's not my fault I'm white,'"[47] Rufo writes, ending with their promise to "'work against systems of oppression' and 'use [their] privilege to support anti-racist work.'"[48]

There are countless additional examples of this process playing out in DEI training across the country. In each case, the "white guilt" psychological conveyor belt is the same: confession, then reeducation. The reeducation phase involves an offer to overcome the pre-confession failings (in this case, being white) with adherence to the right ideology. The broken, guilty mind is harnessed to create true believers.

As you recall, brainwashing requires total debasement of objective truth. The more degrading to previously held beliefs, the better. When the guilty mind now has its foundational beliefs shaken, those beliefs can be replaced entirely. We can see this clearly in diversity training, but the truth is this process is being imposed at every level of culture, including sexuality. Here, for example, a leftist writer rewrites the rules of dating: "Imagine a date that's going well," Brynn Tannehill counsels readers of *The Advocate* in a column titled "Is Refusing to Date Trans People Transphobic?" She goes on:

> There's mutual physical attraction and definite chemistry. Then you find out they're transgender via conversation (yes, everyone still has their clothes on), and end the date right then and there. But for the fact that the other person was transgender, this would have been a really good date, and you probably would have seen them again. This is discrimination against the transgender person for being transgender. Obviously, this isn't illegal, nor should it be. But, from a logical standpoint, yes, this is discriminatory and transphobic.[49]

No person still capable of defending logic, or their fundamental sense of self, would accept the assertion that a man with a penis should be sexually attractive to another heterosexual man, no matter what wig or make up he has on or what plastic surgery procedures he's had done. But "transphobia" has been transformed into such a powerful term that the brainwashed masses avoid it at all costs. It is a cudgel to beat minds into delusion.

To be absolved of all mental sin, they must forgo even the most basic critical thinking about gender and sexuality. They may well feel guilty for having gone through much of their life without considering the needs of the *trans* community—and now, as far as the Left is concerned, it's payback time. To avoid transphobia, one must confess to insufficient allyship in the past and commit to trans absolutism in the future.

Mao would call this a successfully "washed mind."

Communist China policed not only actions but thoughts. They often excused or encouraged actual criminality— murder, rape, robbery—while convincing the mob that the worst crimes were ideas or speech that undermined the narrative of the state. Morality was turned on its head at the direction of the government itself. Good people are made to feel afraid. The violent, collectivist mob, on the other hand, is protected and rewarded.

Totalitarian regimes have a way of codifying these practices. In Iraq, for instance, the jihadists used extreme application of Islamic jurisprudence to create legal legitimacy for their actions.

And in areas of the country where they could achieve enough influence, they set up shadow sharia courts. These temporary, makeshift legal proceedings would often result in torture or execution. For them, the law was a potent tool of psychological manipulation over the population.

I call this form of coercion weaponized law.

4

Weaponized Law

I'd never heard as many police sirens at once as that night in midtown Manhattan.

You could see police cars whipping across the city and the ever-present helicopters above. The choppers gave authorities a bird's-eye view of the chaos below. But it didn't matter. They didn't stop it. Chaos reigned all night.

It was June 1, 2020. Black Lives Matter mobs were rampaging across New York City. They were smashing storefronts and looting merchandise, including on high-end Fifth Avenue, one of the most famous shopping districts in the world. In the name of racial justice, the city of New York had been violated by Black Lives Matter protesters.

I lived right in the thick of the mayhem, on Fifty-Third Street, and could hear the ruckus from my window at all hours.

The next morning, after the mayhem died down, I took a walk around my block to survey the damage. Dozens of store windows were smashed in. Cell phone stores, pharmacies—any unlucky businesses caught in the maelstrom—were ransacked. The BLM hooligans, in their stealing frenzy, left a mess of broken glass, discarded products, and some empty bottles of alcohol behind on the sidewalk across from my building.

Even a small side-street Indian restaurant on the corner of Fifty-Third Street had its glass door kicked in. I remember thinking that the non-white immigrants who owned and operated this family establishment were unlikely to view the destruction of their property as "racial justice."

Innocent people were left defenseless. Law and order had been sacrificed on the altar of wokeness. It was mandatory collective suffering, and it seemed that the powers that be wanted us all to know the fear when a state abandons law to placate deranged mobs.

Where were the police? Over a decade before, I'd spent a year working at the NYPD Intelligence Bureau—so I was quite familiar with the resources and capabilities of America's largest city police force. But the NYPD response was an afterthought for the mobs running rampant. City leadership would later claim to be "overwhelmed" by the thugs. But it would come out, quietly, what we already knew—the BLM marauders were coddled because many of the people in power supported them.

Democrats in charge would go easy on the few who were arrested. Many were even rooting for more mayhem. District attorneys would eventually dismiss these cases en masse. Mayor Bill de Blasio, enamored with the absurd idea that these riots constituted "400 years of racism being addressed,"[1] would make a special exception to his despotic Covid policies so that more BLM marches and riots could occur in defiance of lockdowns.

De Blasio's capriciousness was a stark reminder that, as far as the Left is concerned, the law is whatever they say it is. If you have the right beliefs—their beliefs—you can break the law with impunity. If you don't, stay inside, mask up, keep your distance, and obey.

The whole city—and the world—saw that the June 1 night of anarchy was a sanctioned mobilization of the political Left, in an election year, allowed so a presidential race would be held under threat of force.

But NYC wasn't alone. During that summer of George Floyd in 2020, looters and rioters caused $2 billion in damage across the country in the name of racial justice.[2] Immediately, the media managed the public perception of these events, aiming to paint the hooligans and thieves as activists rather than criminals.

When the riots began in Minneapolis, Minnesota, Craig Melvin tweeted out a warning to his NBC/MSNBC colleagues and viewers, advising them on permissible language: "This will guide our reporting in MN. 'While the situation on the ground in Minneapolis is fluid, and there has been violence, it is most accurate at this time to describe what is happening there as "protests"—not riots.'"[3]

Standing in front of "protesters" destroying Minneapolis, MSNBC's Ali Velshi coached viewers on how they should disbelieve what their eyes were seeing:

> I want to be clear on how I characterize this. This is mostly a protest. It is not, generally speaking, unruly, but fires have been started and this crowd is relishing that. . . . There is a deep sense of grievance and complaint here, and that is the thing. That when you discount people who are doing things to public property that they shouldn't be doing, it does have to be understood that this city has got, for the last several years, an issue with police, and it's got a real sense of the deep sense of grievance of inequality.[4]

This madness continued all summer. "Hundreds of protesters participated in a mostly peaceful march through the streets of downtown Oakland Saturday evening to show support for the ongoing protest continuing in Portland since George Floyd's death nearly two months ago," NBC's Bay Area station reported. "A group later broke off of the mostly peaceful protest and took to vandalism and violence. Oakland Police tweeted that agitators within the group set the Alameda County Courthouse on fire, vandalized the police station and assaulted officers."[5]

This was only the beginning of the live rewriting of history. While reaching inside his car during his August 2020 arrest in Kenosha, Wisconsin, Jacob Blake was shot by police. Then violence ensued. CNN reported, "8PM CURFEW ORDERED AFTER VIOLENT PROTESTS OVER POLICE SHOOTING OF UNARMED BLACK MAN IN WISCONSIN." Five seconds later, CNN stripped out the word "violent."[6] As CNN's correspondent Omar Jimenez reported from Kenosha with a raging fire in the background, the chyron read, "FIERY BUT MOSTLY PEACEFUL PROTESTS AFTER POLICE SHOOTING."[7]

How was it that thousands of rioters were able to maraud through America's city streets in 2020 under the banner of BLM, with so few facing any serious consequences? Yet mere months later, on the other side of politics, January 6 prisoners—Trump voters—languished in DC prisons for over a year, sometimes held in solitary confinement, for entirely nonviolent crimes that had not been proved in a court of law.

What could possibly explain this disparity of treatment under the law?

The former dictator of Peru, Oscar Benavides, offered an answer almost a century ago:

"For my friends everything, for my enemies, the law." That's weaponized law—another way to psychologically beat down dissidents to the system and induce mass hysteria.

Totalitarian "Law": Pure Power

In relatively free societies, we think of the law as a benevolent force. It shapes public behavior from the most minor (traffic violations) to the most extreme (murder). We know that the state is tasked with enforcing this vast set of rules, and ultimately, its ability to do so rests on the use of force. If the laws are moral, clear, and consistently applied, the overall benefit to a society is enormous.

But the law is a tool that can easily be abused. It can even be wielded as a weapon. Taken to extremes, the law can be used for mind control of the masses, coercing immoral behavior and shaping delusional beliefs. In the worst regimes, law can become a tool to elevate sycophants through legal carve-outs and destroy enemies of the powerful through unequal and unjust punishment, dehumanizing both those who are targeted and those who obey.

While there are many variations of weaponized law, its purpose is the same as every other tactic of mass hysteria: power. At its most extreme stage, law becomes whatever the regime claims it to be.

No other justification is needed. Arthur Koestler, in his seminal work, *Darkness at Noon*, made this clear as he wrote that the Soviet regime "knew only one crime: to swerve from the course laid out; and only one punishment: death."[8]

George Orwell's *1984* describes a sequence where an arrested character named Parsons admits that he is guilty of thoughtcrime because the regime of Big Brother would never arrest an innocent man. And beyond that, he might have committed thoughtcrime while sleeping, so there was no point in protesting his innocence. Parsons learned the primary lesson of weaponized law—not to do good and avoid evil, but rather that the regime is always right.[9] In this way, law becomes a psychological weapon. Actions still matter. But what the regime really wants is to end any concept you have of justice and demolish any standards of right and wrong you have outside of what the state says. What the regime wants is control of your thoughts.

Orwell's conception of thoughtcrime describes the reality of totalitarian systems, where you are guilty for wrong thoughts without any burden of proof and without any specific crime cited. Much as how I was automatically deemed problematic at Amherst by virtue of being a straight white male, legal proscriptions and punishments in totalitarian societies are based on the political needs of the system. Actual transgressions of the law or even basic morality are irrelevant. Guilt is instantaneous and inevitable.

Totalitarian rule of law doesn't care about justice or wisdom—the law is a tool of control. Anything can be legal as long as it advances the interests of the regime. In essence, totalitarians assert that the needs of the state are an ultimate law, held above all other considerations. As the famed philosopher of totalitarianism Hannah Arendt said, when this ultimate law is applied, the regime "executes [it] without translating it into standards of right and wrong for individual behavior."[10]

In this way, law can be one of the most effective tools of psychological manipulation and coercion for the individual, and the masses. The totalitarian regimes of the twentieth century proved this over and again. They deployed the law when it suited their rapacious desires for power. They discarded it when the most basic precepts of decency or fairness got in the way. All that matters is the desire of the state.

Under totalitarian regimes, law isn't discarded, it's transformed into something evil.

Few did this more effectively than the Nazis. After World War I, Germany had an intricate, sophisticated legal code that the Nazis never formally abandoned, even during the most heinous years of Hitler's rule. The Nazis transformed German law into a hideous machinery of ethnic repression and genocide, all the while proving that weaponized law is highly effective for controlling minds and fostering mass delusions.

Nazi Weaponization of Law

World War II–era Germany's descent into genocidal hell was a step-by-step process during which the Nazis constantly claimed to have "the law" on their side. Rather than openly erase the legal code, they first embraced it, then co-opted it, and finally corrupted it to its core. The Nazis knew the power of weaponized law to attack enemies and excuse the most flagrant, inhumane depredations. At every stage, there were Germans who were able to ignore or justify their own behaviors as "legal," no matter how immoral.

In fact, the Third Reich always maintained the pretense that the Weimar Constitution remained in effect. There was never a National Socialist Constitution, though the Nazi leadership considered drafting one.[11] They preferred to abuse the existing legal framework beyond recognition.

The Nazi desire to appeal to traditional Germanic legalism could be seen in some of their earliest anti-Jewish legislation. When the Nazis declared that the Jews could no longer legally slaughter animals by kosher means, they presented themselves as crusaders against unnecessary animal cruelty.[12] When the Nazis made it illegal for Jews to change their names, they did so under the justification that Jewish name changes were intended to deceive the public, and therefore it was necessary to ban the practice.[13]

Then the Nazis—under the guise of concern for public health—banned Jews from entering public swimming pools, as any contact with a Jewish body would pollute the water.[14] The laws at first slowly escalated and restricted Jewish freedoms until, by the end of their terror, the Nazis passed over 1,900 examples of "special Jewish law[s]."[15]

Almost everyone familiar with the Second World War knows about the brutal SS Einsatzgruppen, infamous for killing prisoners in mass graves that they themselves had dug.[16] But the SS were far from the only enforcers of Nazi tyranny. As Hans-Christian Jasch writes, "Hannah Arendt coined the term 'banality of evil' to describe the 'clerks' in the service of genocide."[17] There was even a term for the functionaries who helped the Nazis leverage the existing bureaucracy for their plans— *Schreibtischtäter* ("desk perpetrators").[18]

The German civil service would become a critical tool of Hitler's monstrous rule. And it all started when the Nazis seized control of the legal apparatus, from writing laws to controlling those who implemented the law.

The Nazis began in 1933 by targeting what they viewed as the insidious overrepresentation of Jews in the German legal profession (around 30 percent of all lawyers in some parts of the country).[19] They banned Jewish lawyers and notaries from doing any business with or in the name of the state. In short order, by the end of 1933, the German government declared that "non-Aryans cannot be appointed as either lay judges or jury members."[20]

By late 1938, all Jewish lawyers were formally disbarred except for those who took on the role of Jewish Konsulent (adviser).[21]

With the Jews out and all other lawyers put on notice, Hitler began bending the legal system to his will, including making lawyers complicit in the Final Solution, the mass murder of six million Jews. Functionaries who wanted to rise within the ranks of the Third Reich focused on issues related to the harassment, imprisonment, and eventual extermination of the Jews.

After the war, a legal reckoning came to Germany. Much like the well-known Nuremberg trials that ended in October 1946, the United States conducted a total of twelve postwar trials in occupied zones in order to hold members of the Nazi apparatus accountable for their crimes.[22]

One of these trials was called the Justice Case,[23] which basically put the Nazi legal system on trial. Members of the judiciary under the Nazi regime were charged with using the law as an "instrument of brutality and terror."[24]

The defendants argued that they were merely functionaries operating at the behest of the Führer—which in their position meant they were merely following the law. The entire Nazi regime operated under a doctrine they officially called *Führerprinzip*—distilled into "the will of the Führer is the party's law," and "the

Führer is always right."[25] Their defense was farcical. It revealed that rule of law in Nazi Germany was pure propaganda. The real driving force behind the justice system was the political needs or whims of Hitler and his organs of state security—the ultimate law. The court saw through the smoke screen, and many judges and prosecutors were convicted, with some facing imprisonment and prosecution.

Hitler's Bloodthirsty Court

But it wasn't enough for Hitler to take over the existing legal structure. The Nazis also established an independent court to more aggressively impose Nazi ideology on the entire population. In 1934, Chancellor Hitler established the *Volksgerichtshof* (acronym VGH, for "People's Court"). Officially, the court was meant to handle "high treason, state treason, . . . preparation for treason, undermining national defense . . . , and favoring the enemy," as Robert D. Rachlin describes it.[26]

In reality, the VGH had a broad mandate that invited the most arbitrary, politicized judgments and often imposed death for crimes unmentioned in the German legal code. This included a regular practice of criminalizing acts after they were committed and that had before never been treated as illegal. In this, they dispensed with the millennia-old Roman legal principle of *Nullum crimin sine lege*—no crime without a law. The law was whatever the Nazi judges said it was.

In fact, the VGH was so vicious in its judgments in the early years that some high-level Nazis were concerned it would undermine their attempts to appear—at least superficially—like a law-and-order society. It is estimated that Hitler's VGH court ordered more than 5,200 executions during its eleven-year existence, including for shockingly minor offenses.[27] According to Rachlin:

> A priest was sentenced to death for telling a joke about a soldier who had been gravely wounded and asked to see the faces of the people for whom he was about to die. A picture of Hitler was placed on his right, a picture of Göring on his left. The soldier then remarked that he was dying like Christ.[28]

The VGH in 1942 sentenced a German iron worker to death for anti-regime graffiti he wrote on the inside of a toilet stall.[29] That same year, the court tried a student for giving out anti-war leaflets. He was sentenced to death and beheaded via guillotine.[30] Atrocities like this continued all throughout the Nazis' reign.

The psychic impact of the VGH was profound. In the 1930s,

Germany had a population of roughly seventy million people, meaning the VGH executed only a fraction of a percent of the German population. But the randomness and post-facto nature of the court's decisions made every German feel vulnerable. The average German citizen wasn't left alone simply because he wasn't a Jew. He was made to be afraid of ever contradicting the regime and to have his spirit of opposition broken.

The VGH helped accomplish those goals and made space for the mass delusion of Nazism to spread. In a way, it was like suicide bombing in the war on terror. It didn't matter if more people died from other causes, like in gunfights or from IEDs. The randomness of the suicide bombings, like the randomness of VGH rulings, created terror that made the population more pliable and capable of being controlled.

The VGH coupled with the breakneck speed at which laws were being changed to target Jews, Roma (Gypsies), and other groups left the entire population disoriented. This weakened the will of those who resisted the Nazi political machine and left them with fewer options to fight back or slow down changes within the existing system.

The Nazi takeover of the legal system also helps to explain how it's possible that so many millions of Germans were complicit in—or indifferent to—Nazi atrocities. By harnessing the legal code to mandate discrimination, Hitler's minions stained the consciences of countless everyday Germans who were given the opportunity to "follow the law," no matter how unjust and vile.

All of this was possible because Hitler's law supplanted right and wrong and turned justice into a weapon of terror.

"Social Justice": Criminals as the Protected Class

Where Nazi law was evil because it proactively mandated wrongdoing and punished good, weaponized law for the most part operates differently in America. It's not necessarily about whom the law punishes here; it's about whom it refuses to punish. As I said before, law shapes people—both in what it restricts and in what it allows. And the truth is, both perversions of law manipulate people's conception of right and wrong and entrench a state of mass delusion.

It happened to me. Heck, in a certain way I was born into a state of mass delusion. Let me explain.

I remember when I was mugged for the first time. I was twelve years old, a street thug demanded all my money, and I gave my wallet over. It was Velcro and had maybe five dollars in it. Hardly worth the possibility of arrest and prosecution for robbery.

But this was New York City in the early 1990s. Crime like this was so constant, it wasn't even worth reporting to the police.

It was just my turn to get mugged, as seemingly everyone had. Even if the robber was caught, nothing would happen to him anyway.

My elementary school had to hire a guard—on swanky East Eighty-Ninth Street in Carnegie Hill—to stop the countless muggings that were occurring *right out in front of the school.* You'd walk out of class, some degenerates in a pack would surround you, punch you, and walk off with your Walkman. The thugs expected no consequences, and they were almost always right.

In the 1990s, there were convicts running rampant around New York City who had been arrested *hundreds* of times. Decay and despair were observable everywhere. Graffiti was a visual virus that had spread throughout every borough, including the wealthiest areas. There was a full-blown homeless encampment on the street, next to a synagogue, immediately around the corner from my family's apartment building on Manhattan's wealthy Upper East Side. I recall my father once getting into an argument with a vagrant who was urinating on our building's front step on an otherwise lovely Sunday evening in the Big Apple.

But public urination was the least of our worries. New Yorkers knew it was too dangerous to venture into Central Park at night alone. If you went for an evening stroll in the park— among the most famous urban green spaces in the world—and got robbed, the general attitude was "well, you shouldn't go there at night."

The threat of serious crime in any neighborhood, at any time, was very real. It's hard to believe now, but New York City had 2,262 murders, 3,126 rapes, and more than 100,000 robberies in 1990 alone.[31] It appeared that low-scale anarchy was just the way the world was. At my age, I couldn't think of New York in any other way.

And then the miracles of Mayor Rudy Giuliani began when he took office in 1994. Under his leadership, New Yorkers broke free of their mandatory delusion that crime couldn't be stopped, or that its root cause was poverty. Giuliani showed that when you increase police presence, empower them to arrest criminals, and aggressively prosecute crimes—including low-level crimes—shockingly, crime declines. Giuliani broke the mass psychosis that reigned in New York, where everyone presumed crime was just a part of city life. Order finally triumphed over mass criminality.

By the time I graduated from Regis High School, a few blocks from where I had been mugged years before, the city was an entirely different place. The 2,262 annual murders were brought down to 673 in 2000 (continuing downward to an all-time low of 292 in 2017).[32] I felt safe anywhere in Manhattan at any time of the day or night. Women, including in my own family, could go jogging in Central Park hours after sundown with no fear. In college, when I would come home to New York, I could stumble out of nightclubs in lower Manhattan at three in the morning and never worry about getting robbed.

The air of perpetual menace was gone.

From that young age, I noticed that when it came to crime and punishment, people who made "liberal" arguments about crime were simply delusional and far more interested in convincing their friends of their goodness than keeping anyone safe. What's worse, they made everyone else delusional, too, imagining that parroting lines about "structural inequality," "root causes," and "ending mass incarceration" could replace arresting criminals and actually punishing them for their crimes.

Thankfully, after Giuliani came on the scene, the anti-crime voices in America were ascendant. It was a glorious revolution that saved tens of thousands of lives and spared millions of Americans from assault, theft, and the harassment of petty crime.

But left-wing delusion never went away. One generation of peace gave ideologues the space to promote the same psychotic pro-crime philosophy that caused all our problems in the first place. It really began to take off again when Barack Obama was elected president in 2008. Many believed that his election would bring about a racial healing. Obama's sweeping electoral victory exemplified the tremendous progress America had made since the evils of slavery and Jim Crow. We finally had a black president. True racial harmony was surely just around the corner.

Alas, race relations moved in the opposite direction. Obama was a talented demagogue, all too happy to shut down his critics with bad-faith insinuations or outright allegations of racism. And he would use this tactic to inflame and exploit racial tensions for political gain. In one example of this pandering, Obama singled out a few of the original supposed martyrs of the BLM movement, telling Black Entertainment Television (BET) back in December of 2014:

> If you look at after what happened with Michael Brown, if you looked at what happened after Trayvon, if you looked at the decision after Eric Garner, I'm being pretty explicit about my concern, and being pretty explicit about the fact that this is a systemic problem, that black folks and Latinos and others are not just making this up.[33]

Obama knew the game he was playing. Trayvon Martin was shot by George Zimmerman, a Hispanic man, in self-defense, as, Zimmerman claims, Martin shoved Zimmerman to the ground and repeatedly smashed his head into the concrete sidewalk. In his trial, Zimmerman was found not guilty.

Eric Garner refused police commands, a police officer tackled him to the ground in a choke hold, and Garner died from a combination of heart failure, asthma, and asphyxiation.[34] The officer involved was fired for using a prohibited choke hold, but no fair-minded person thinks he meant to kill Garner and destroy his career and life in the process.

Michael Brown was killed in August 2014 while approaching Darren Wilson, a police officer who had his firearm drawn and told Brown to stop. Obama's own DOJ, with Attorney General Eric Holder in charge, found Wilson used lethal force in self-defense. There were multiple eyewitnesses to the incident who supported Wilson's account—and they were themselves black.

Further, none of these cases were indicative of a larger trend. The number of black Americans unlawfully killed by police in any given year is very small. *The Washington Post*, for example, has a database tracking these incidents, and it found fourteen incidents in 2019, before the BLM 2.0 movement of 2020 began.[35]

Obama ignored the facts of each case and the facts about so-called systemic racism. But that was part of the point. If people could be made to believe that facts don't matter, only race . . . well, it's exactly like convincing people that facts don't matter, only class. Might makes right. The law is determined by who has the power to define the good people versus the bad people. When that happens, we've taken one more step closer to a totalitarian concept of law.

Obama was encouraging mass delusion in what looked like a pure power play. The BLM movement was underway. Obama chose to bolster the belief that police in America systematically target and murder unarmed black men for no reason but racial hatred, presumably because much of his political power was based on racial conflict. He may have thought that people who believed this lie would vote for Democrats—and for Obama—because they posed as the ones fighting injustice.

Years after Obama—and after the politicized prosecutions of Trump—the American people are still left wondering if our legal system is truly fair, or if what really matters is who has the power to decide right and wrong. We're trending a bad direction, but the jury is still out.

In America, abuse of the law is not at totalitarian levels yet, thankfully.

But we have seen unprecedented weaponization of the law. Over time, the Left has embraced an "ultimate law" framework, giving the green light to that which attacks their enemies while unfairly using the law to protect favored political classes.

This has a psychological impact on every American.

Special Counsel Robert Mueller spent two years trying to find evidence that Trump's 2016 presidential campaign colluded with the Russians and obstructed justice during the investigation. Whatever your opinion of Donald Trump, everyone can hear the echo of Soviet Communist Secret Police Chief Lavrentiy Beria's claim "Show me the man, I'll show you the crime" in Mueller. Instead of innocent until proven guilty, Mueller said at the end of the investigation: "If we had had confidence that the president clearly did not commit a crime, we would have said so,"[36] claiming the report did not exonerate him. The process, of course, was the punishment.

Other partisan prosecutors have grossly weaponized law. Alvin Bragg, the Manhattan DA who refuses to indict street criminals, prosecuted Trump for alleged violations of campaign-finance laws—federal crimes that Bragg has no business pursuing. Of course, the Manhattan DA brought no charges against Hillary Clinton—Trump's 2016 opponent—who was fined by the Federal Election Commission after her campaign hid its funding of bogus Russian collusion research provided to the FBI. In fact, no federal prosecutor explored whether Clinton had committed a felony.[37]

This type of lawfare has been going on for years. One side is punished unfairly—the other excused unjustly. When the FBI discovered Hillary Clinton had mishandled very sensitive, highly classified information as secretary of state, then FBI Director

James Comey declined to pursue charges: "Although there is evidence of potential violations regarding the handling of classified information, our judgment is that no reasonable prosecutor would bring such a case," he said.[38] I had a top secret clearance in the CIA, and if I ran hundreds of classified documents over my private server in some scheme to evade public record laws, prison time would have almost assuredly been in my future.

Ah, but then look at how the enemies of the regime are treated. For (in many cases non-violently) protesting inside the US Capitol on January 6, 2021, at least 327 Trump supporters have been charged with "obstruction of an official proceeding"—and face up to twenty years in prison upon conviction.[39] Those who assaulted officers faced the fullest weight of the law. In fact, they were punished far more vigorously than others charged with similar crimes. The FBI tracked them down and raided their homes, often with the help of a group calling themselves "sedition hunters," comprised of volunteers who were motivated in no small part by their desire to destroy political enemies. Trump's pardons for January 6 individuals in January 2025 took all of this weaponization into account.

This trend of the Left's using the state to destroy perceived political enemies has been building for a long time, and it overwhelmingly goes in one direction. There was the special counsel "leak" investigation of the Bush administration, ensnaring I.

Lewis "Scooter" Libby on a technicality, but apparently intended to imprison Karl Rove. Partisan prosecutors abused the law to investigate or indict former governors Scott Walker of Wisconsin, Rick Perry of Texas, Chris Christie of New Jersey, and Bob McDonnell of Virginia. In each case, the most aggressive investigative and prosecutorial tactics possible were used, and no crimes appear to have been committed (though with McDonnell, the Supreme Court had to step in and undo a conviction).

Most infamously of all, the so-called Russia collusion case against Trump, and the four separate criminal indictments brought against him leading up to the 2024 election year, are the clearest evidence yet that we are sliding toward the weaponized law of a totalitarian state.

That the political Left acts to simultaneously minimize or ignore law enforcement efforts against a whole range of real offenses—illegal immigration, violent crime, robberies, theft, quality-of-life offenses—shows what the real game is: You are to suffer from criminals, without protection of the law, when they politically benefit from it. And if you cross them politically, the full effect of the law will be brought down on your head.

They are pursuing an ultimate law of total power.

Justice is not their goal. Fear is.

And when that manipulated fear becomes so deeply ingrained that it controls mind, we have a term for it.

Forced phobia.

5

Forced Phobia

Dread shot through me one Saturday night in Manhattan in the spring of 2010. A message on my NYPD-issued BlackBerry told me that only a short distance away, smoke was pouring out of an SUV that was packed with explosives and abandoned in Times Square.

A mass-casualty terror attack had been narrowly averted—not by the good guys, but by sheer luck.

Faisal Shahzad—a naturalized American citizen from Pakistan now serving life in prison—calmly walked to Grand Central Terminal as he waited for his car bomb to detonate (thankfully, it ultimately failed). He rode the train back to his home in suburban Connecticut. Shahzad was married with children, had an MBA from the University of Bridgeport, and worked as an account analyst. He reportedly grew up with a taste for the finer things, sponging off his parents in one of Pakistan's posh neighborhoods.[1] Shahzad was seduced by the Salafi strain of Islam, which blames non-believers for polluting the purity of the seventh-century Sunni caliphate in Medina. In Pakistan, he was injected with fear—fear that the West was corrupting Islam, fear that the "Crusaders" were murdering his people. In his mind, Islam was under assault, and if he didn't do something to stop it, his Muslim brothers and sisters were going to die.

Now Shahzad saw a chance to trade his fear for power.

Pleading guilty to ten counts of terrorism to a federal judge, Shahzad maintained, "I am part of the answer to the US terrorizing the Muslim nations. I'm avenging the attacks because the Americans only care about their people, but they don't care about the people elsewhere in the world when they die. . . . We Muslims are one community. We're not divided."[2]

It wasn't just shame-induced fear driving Islamic radicalism. In Africa, Iraq, and Afghanistan, I watched Muslims terrifying one another into compliance with horrific acts of violence and fearmongering about the threats of the West. Shahzad's parents' village was repeatedly struck by Taliban suicide bombers. Hemmed in by fear of reprisals on one side and fear of a great enemy on the other, Shahzad apparently broke. If he believed what he was telling the judge, Shahzad's mind had been hijacked by fear.

There are hundreds—thousands—of potential Shahzads walking around New York and other American cities, translating their own fear into public terror. And all it takes is one successful, catastrophic attack to kill scores of innocents. My role with the NYPD's Intelligence Division that year was to monitor how and why ordinary individuals with no criminal history try to commit acts of terrorism. I learned that, in the early stages of radicalization, their brains are usually hijacked by fear.

And that total mind control is impossible without weaponizing fear.

The Consequences of Fear

What happens in a society where the people live in perpetual dread?

We know from modern psychiatry that fear is powerful enough to change the brain. Scientists have studied the chemical effects on brains from soldiers' war zone deployments, including in a 2021 study of PTSD involving 120 German soldiers that observed changes in brain structure.[3] This didn't come from physical trauma to the brain, as is the case with soldiers who suffer from traumatic brain injury. The MRI scans showed that soldiers who had merely witnessed traumatic events in war zones had suffered physiologically identifiable trauma to their brains. Obviously fear is a powerful stimulus.

Accounts from those who have lived in totalitarian states capture the fear they felt daily, and many—like the North Korean defector Yeonmi Park—were later diagnosed with PTSD. Their stories highlight not only the lifelong effects of fear but also how fear makes them more vulnerable to coercion and even delusion. After all, people who are afraid look for a way out; they want something—or someone—to make everything right again. They want someone to destroy what they have been taught to hate. A mind at peace is hard to crack. A mind taken over by fear is ripe for manipulation.

Sociopaths, cult leaders, and megalomaniacs see fear as an opportunity to achieve power. To them, traumatized people are not victims but prey. Strategic trauma can turn everyday citizens into monsters. First you terrify everyone; then you promise the frightened masses that they will be safe, as long as they do what they're told.

Take, for example, the French Revolution. In the late eighteenth century, the French Revolution was the most fashionable cause on earth—comparable to today's "anti-colonial" Palestinian uprising. Coming on the heels of the American Revolution, the overthrow of Louis XVI and the ancient French monarchy seemed to herald a new era of human liberation from oppression. In this case, the oppressor was not colonialism but monarchism. The revolution's slogan was "Liberté, égalité, fraternité!"

It quickly turned into a bloodbath. The revolution's machinery of violence created such a state of fear, it would come to be known simply as "La Terreur," the Terror.

At Paris's Revolutionary Tribunal of 1793, "victims were shepherded to the courtroom in the morning. . . . By three o'clock, their hair had been cut, their hands bound and they were in the death carts on their way to the scaffold," writes Stanley Loomis.[4] As the philosopher and historian John Kekes noted, "Most of these people were innocent of any crime and were unable to defend themselves against accusations of which they were not even informed."[5]

One of those accused was Princess de Lamballe, a friend and relative of the royal family. After refusing to swear her hatred of her family members, the princess was handed over to the bloodthirsty mob: "She was dispatched with a pike thrust, her still beating heart was ripped from her body and devoured, her legs and arms were severed from her body and shot through cannon. . . . "The horrors that were then perpetrated on her disemboweled torso are indescribable," writes Loomis.[6]

In Lyon, "as many as sixty prisoners were tied in a line by ropes and shot at with cannon," writes Simon Schama.[7] In Nantes, holes were cut into the sides of boats, "prisoners were put in with their hands and feet tied and the boats were pushed into the center of the river" so "victims helplessly watched the water rise about them."[8] Sometimes this technique would be performed on a hand-selected couple, who were first stripped naked and tied up together. This became known as a "Republican marriage."

The Vendée region in western France, a center of Catholic resistance to the Revolution, became home to what has been described as the world's first "ideological genocide," according to the historian Pierre Chaunu. Simon Schama says of the republican violence that claimed the lives of two hundred thousand people, "Every atrocity the time could imagine was meted out to the defenseless population."[9]

"Women were routinely raped, children killed, both mutilated," Schama writes.[10] In short order, more than two hundred thousand Frenchmen and women were imprisoned, some ten thousand of whom died in jail. Formal executions were so frequent, crowded, and geographically dispersed that historians can only guess at a total number somewhere between sixteen thousand and forty thousand. We do know that at the height of its power, the Revolutionary Tribunal—described by one historian as an "undiscriminating murder machine"[11]—executed an average of thirty-six people per day.[12]

The French people were so traumatized by the Jacobins that they not only accepted but celebrated the violence of the revolution. Or if they didn't celebrate the revolution, they at least became so terrified that they learned to keep quiet. There was nothing that could stop the revolutionary leaders' zeal in arbitrarily arresting innocent citizens, guillotining them by the thousands, directing drunken mobs to rape nuns, disembowel priests, cannibalize princesses, and torture children. They all "believed themselves motivated by patriotic and altruistic impulses" and "value[d] their good intentions more highly than human life," writes Loomis.[13] The revolutionaries had no empathy for the terrified people because they were being terrorized for their own good. Loomis goes on to describe the totalitarian morality this way: "There is no crime, no murder, no massacre that cannot be justified, provided it be committed in the name of an Ideal."[14]

When the horrors of the revolution erased traditional notions of good and evil, the traumatized people latched onto a new set of ideals. We can see how fear is a crucial part of our previous discussion on mind control, because fear created a blank slate upon which the revolutionaries could impose their own ideology to entrench and expand their power. Kekes adds that this "justification of monstrous actions by appealing to a passionately held ideal" would become the defining hallmark of every totalitarian ideology to come: Communism, fascism, Nazism, Islamist terrorism, and the rest.[15] In every case, the ideology's ideal was elevated above and "immune from rational or moral criticism, because it determines what is reasonable and moral."[16]

Fear of the guillotine is rational if you're living in Revolutionary France. But not all of the fears that totalitarian regimes instill in their citizens are rational. Irrational fear is a phobia—you might recall common phobias like those of small spaces, spiders, and crowds. And the most heinous tyrants love to use irrational phobias against their people.

The cult expert Steven Hassan calls this tactic—whereby tyrants wield irrational fear against their people—"phobia indoctrination," and described it as "the single most powerful technique for keeping people dependent and obedient."[17] In the wrong hands, a phobia is a psychic leash that can be used to guide and choke the mind of a fearful individual or group. Recall, for example, the Germans' phobia of the Jewish germs under the Nazi regime. It was an irrational fear that opened the possibility for murderous results.

On a smaller scale, we can see irrational phobia indoctrination in the development of cults.

Some of the most infamous cults of the past seventy years—Heaven's Gate, the Branch Davidians, the Peoples Temple (all of which ended in massacres, either self-inflicted or induced)—leveraged the extreme fears of their followers to command obedience. For example, in the Peoples Temple, the cult leader Jim Jones convinced his followers that nuclear war was imminent and that the government was constantly spying on them, threatening them, and even trying to murder him. Without that steady (and steadily increasing) dosage of fear, I doubt his followers would have moved to the godforsaken jungles of South America, where they ultimately met their doom.

Cult indoctrination generally moves along a standard process that mirrors what Robert Jay Lifton discovered in his interviews with Chinese Communist brainwashing victims. I studied this myself. On their way to true-believer status, most homegrown Islamist terrorists go through the stages of isolation (another subject we'll cover with more depth in the next chapter), indoctrination, group affirmation, and then punishment for disobedience.

We might think of cult victims, as described by Dr. Hassan, as usually harmless, lost people with minds of mush, but phobia indoctrination can have global consequences. After all, manipulation of mass phobia has led to decades of war in the Middle East against jihadist enemies who claim to love death more than we love life. But fear is also weaponized in less obvious ways and by far less powerful individuals and groups. In the modern West today, for example, there are no guillotines lopping off heads in the town square. Governments are far less willing to engage in mass violence against their own populations. But fear remains a potent tool, enabled by constant media saturation of our minds. And charismatic leaders remain capable of inspiring fear in their subjects based on conspiracies and delusions. What is one common way these leaders wield control over our minds without the extreme force of totalitarian regimes?

They fixate on the end of the world as we know it.

Weaponizing Extinction Anxiety

Everyone is going to die. That we humans have foreknowledge of our eventual demise separates us from all other species. In many ways this awareness can be beneficial to us.

At an evolutionary level, fear of death is a helpful tool for our survival. Our brains constantly remind us: Don't drive the car too fast or you may spin out and hit a tree. If you smell smoke in the middle of the night at home, it's a good thing for your heart to start racing. Fear and our survival mechanisms are intertwined at the most instinctual level. The pesky little amygdala is our friend.

But what we see today is a slew of charlatans and delusional causes hijacking the fear centers of brains. In the modern context, this has given rise to what Andy Kessler of *The Wall Street Journal* called "extinction anxiety."[18] Kessler picked up on the recent trend, amplified on social media, of analysis that the human species could be wiped out entirely in the years or decades ahead.

These extinction anxieties take a variety of forms. The most recent cause for mass panic is the fear that artificial intelligence will bring about the extinction of humanity. Covid-19 has also heightened fears that pandemic disease could end up eradicating all humans.

Extinction fears are not new. One prominent version of them whose influence can still be seen today began almost two hundred years ago. In 1798, the economist and social scientist Thomas Robert Malthus argued that population grows geometrically, while food production is arithmetic.[19] This led him to assert that eventually population would outstrip food production, and the resultant famine and death would cause an overall population decline.

Obviously, Malthus was wrong. The global population was estimated at around one billion near the turn of the nineteenth century, when he wrote his *Essay on the Principle of Population*. It has rocketed to around eight billion people today. But Malthus was unable to foresee the technological advances that made this possible—for example, industrially produced fertilizers and steam engines.

Despite Malthus's errors, Malthusian theory was used to justify monstrous political decisions, such as the British government's response to the Irish potato famine of 1840. The government believed it was better for the poor peasants of Ireland to die off, as it was an "effective mechanism for reducing surplus population."[20] Malthusian ideas provided a foundation for the eugenics movement that would become ideologically fashionable (and occasionally implemented) in Europe and the Americas around the turn of the twentieth century.

Malthus's arguments found a new audience in 1968, when a bug-and-plant expert in the Stanford University biology department named Paul Ehrlich published a book called *The Population Bomb*. The first sentence of that book reads: "The battle to feed all of humanity is over," and goes on to argue that "hundreds of millions of people will starve to death."[21]

While the book initially failed to garner much attention, eventually Ehrlich was able to get on *The Tonight Show Starring Johnny Carson* in February 1970.[22] His appearance created such a stir with the public that NBC decided to have him back again on the show in April of that year. Ehrlich went on to sell millions of copies of his book. Like Malthus before him, he had tapped into the fear center of the public's brain.

Just as with Malthus, there were negative real-life consequences from this epidemic of fear, sparking a new movement to limit global population. Massive population die-off predicted by a lack of food production never occurred. But Ehrlich so convinced people that this fear was real that there were efforts to limit population before food could run out. Millions of people around the world in the 1970s and 1980s were forcibly sterilized or made to undergo abortions. China's infamous one-child policy is perhaps the most egregious example. Its population cratered and now its Communist regime hurries to reverse course. In the Philippines, birth-control pills were dropped out of helicopters above villages to slow population growth.[23]

Sometimes the experts just get it wrong. Malthus and Ehrlich may well have believed their theories when they wrote them. But whether they are true believers or not, those who peddle politicized scientific ideologies can be incredibly effective at exploiting extinction fears to mobilize mass movements.

For one thing: These fears are perpetual. Those who wish to manipulate the minds of the masses can decry the threat of excess population all day, every day, and they can never be proved wrong. If the predicted ecological catastrophe fails to occur, all the charlatans need to do is to push the timeline out a few more years (or decades).

These extinction fears are also intentionally exaggerated. As a result, they have an even more severe impact on the brains of those who fall victim to them. Extinction anxiety is such a powerful force in politics because it goes beyond what any reasonable person would worry about. It's one thing to be stressed about being able to pay your mortgage after a job loss. That's a reasonable manifestation of anxiety. But what happens to the mind when it becomes obsessed with the eradication of our species? Anything that can stop it seems reasonable. Any cost is worth paying to avoid the catastrophe.

When people believe that the apocalypse is near, their minds become vulnerable to hijacking. Once someone has become convinced they're on a mission to save the world, nothing of equivalent importance exists to counterbalance their goal. To save the world, any insane idea is justified—which is exactly what has happened in the climate change movement.

The Climate Change Cult

"You have stolen my dreams and my childhood with your empty words. And yet I'm one of the lucky ones. People are suffering. People are dying. Entire ecosystems are collapsing. We are in the beginning of a mass extinction, and all you can talk about is money and fairy tales of eternal economic growth. *How dare you!* [emphasis added]."[24]

In September 2019, climate activists at the United Nations Climate Action Summit had chosen Greta Thunberg, a sixteen-year-old Swedish teenager on strike from attending high school, as their avatar of climate emergency.

Thunberg and her parents admit that, in addition to having Asperger's syndrome (which she calls her "superpower"), she was diagnosed as a child with obsessive-compulsive disorder, selective mutism, and an eating disorder. When she was eight, she was introduced to climate change catastrophe theories and spiraled down a rabbit hole of irrational fear. Thunberg went on strike from high school to raise attention, demanded her opera singer mother cease air travel (which her career depended on), started taking trains and carbon-neutral boats around the world, and told other countries how to run their economies.

That a teenager with severe anxiety and autism—but no formal scientific education—would freak out over the end of the world and try to control her parents and everyone else is not remarkable. What is remarkable is the mass delusion of the adults who gave her a global platform and treated her like a child oracle. She was feted on CNN and MSNBC and treated with the utmost seriousness by many in the media and among those pushing climate agendas. In 2019 she was named *Time's* "Person of the Year."

Standing before the United Nations, Thunberg derided as insufficient a proposed 50 percent emissions reduction over the course of ten years, claiming it would give the world only a 50 percent chance of preventing the global average temperature from rising more than 1.5 degrees Celsius, a goal set in the 2016 Paris Agreement, which says that "crossing the 1.5°C threshold risks unleashing far more severe climate change impacts, including more frequent and severe droughts, heatwaves and rainfall."[25]

Since the chance that the most populous countries on earth will cut their emissions in half this decade is precisely zero, we're supposedly doomed anyway.

More important, *why was everyone still listening to this child and applauding her?* With her "superpowers" and youthful rage,

Greta Thunberg makes a more inspiring spiritual guru than environmentalist and former vice president Al Gore. But nobody with common sense would give her the time of day. More likely, she was welcomed into the public debate because those in power were so afraid (or at least so eager to stoke fear) of climate catastrophe that they were willing to take hold of any ecological avatar.

For those who bought into this, fear made them blind. Just as Faisal Shahzad and other homegrown radicals I tracked should've been smart enough to see that the Muslim world is not one victimized religion united against evil Western aggressors, Greta Thunberg's fawning admirers ought to know that the "consensus" on climate change has been consistently, repeatedly wrong over the past fifty years.

Way back in 1970, *The Boston Globe* ran a story with the headline, "Scientist Predicts a New Ice Age by 21st Century."

"Air pollution," the story read, "may obliterate the sun and cause a new ice age in the first third of the next century."[26]

Two years later, leftist geology professors at Brown University predicted a new ice age. "The present rate of cooling," they wrote, "seems fast enough to bring glacial temperatures in about a century, if continuing at the present pace."[27]

Time and *The Washington Post* dutifully promoted the story, too.[28]

The New York Times was even more hysterical. In 1978, they were late to the old-and-busted global freeze party ("International Team of Specialists Finds No End in Sight to 30-Year Cooling Trend in Northern Hemisphere").[29] But a year later, they were out in front on the new hotness: "Climatologists Are Warned North Pole Might Melt."[30] Global cooling was out; global warming was in.

In 1988, climate activists predicted the Maldives Islands could be uninhabitable *within thirty years*.

In 1989, the Associated Press hyped predictions by a United Nations environment analyst that "entire nations could be wiped off the face of the earth by rising sea levels if global warming is not reversed by the year 2000."[31]

In 2000, the *Independent* published an article claiming that "snow is starting to disappear from our lives."[32]

In 2004, the US Defense Department reported to President Bush that by 2020, the UK's weather would "resemble Siberia" and the Netherlands would be uninhabitable because of violent storms destroying sea barriers.[33]

In 2006, former vice president Al Gore declared, "The North Pole will be ice-free in the Summer by 2013 because of manmade global warming."[34] That same year, NBC reported on a scientist's prediction that we had just a "ten-year window" to avoid global catastrophes.[35]

In 2009, John Kerry—who would become President Biden's climate czar—promoted yet another doomsday prediction:

"Scientists project that the Arctic will be ice-free in the summer of 2013."[36]

And in 2018, Greta Thunberg was already a global superstar when she tweeted, "A top climate scientist is warning that climate change will wipe out all of humanity unless we stop using fossil fuels over the next five years."[37] Like every other doomsday warning Miss Thunberg has since proclaimed, this prophecy was greeted with cheers from activists and solidarity from the media. But of course, it's been more than five years since she posted that prediction—and we're still here.

There are literally thousands of such predictions tying climate change to imminent famine, plague, starvation, dislocation, and disease. Every time a natural disaster hits, you can be sure that those in power will point to climate change (as if the world didn't have hurricanes before). A rational person only has to look at the record and realize that alarmism is a ruse. But most people don't know that. Young people, especially, hear the climate change catastrophe narrative from nearly every institutional source they know: school, the news media, corporate marketing, and celebrity activism. For some, it can seem like *everyone* they trust is issuing apocalyptic warnings 24/7.

If climate-phobic narratives were remotely true, people would be right to respond with fear, anxiety, panic, and even a step toward political extremism. And that's the point. Climate catastrophism is not run-of-the-mill political activism, like "No new taxes!" or "Raise the minimum wage!" It's a campaign of terrifying lies. Yet the climate liars enthusiastically justify their dishonesty because of the high political ideals they are trying to advance of a "cleaner" and more "just" world.

It strains credulity that they really thought the Maldives would be submerged by now or London would be under permafrost by 2020. It's much more likely they believed their environmental agenda—socializing oil companies, banning drilling, restricting air travel, restricting meat consumption, and the rest—was *so virtuous* and *so important* it justified scaring two generations of credulous citizens out of their wits. It's reasonable to conclude, then, these people know they can only achieve the power they desire if people are submissive and obedient because of their fear.

More moderate rhetoric and modest ambitions would probably win the Left greater support for carbon-mitigation policies. But tinkering with humdrum laws governing urban planning, daylight saving time, and nuclear energy wouldn't serve the Left's messianic ideology—nor would it give them power to tell you what you can eat, where you can travel, and how hot you can keep your house.

Sanity would allow voters to make rational choices about priorities and advance democratic deliberation. That would be good enough for sincere reformers. But for fanatics it will never be good enough—so they conjure apocalyptic stories to terrify their countrymen into submission . . . and inspire a small percentage of the country to become enforcers of the elite's quasi-religious environmentalist goals.

Anxiety about the fate of the planet has taken a toll on the modern psyche. A few shocking statistics from a 2021 survey of sixteen- to twenty-five-year-olds across ten countries points to a massive cognitive hijacking:

- Fifty-nine percent of respondents were very—or extremely—worried about climate change.

- More than half reported each of the following emotions: sadness, anxiety, anger, powerlessness, helplessness, and guilt.

- Over 45 percent said climate-related emotions had an impact on their day-to-day functioning.

- Seventy-five percent said that they were frightened by the future.[38]

A 2023 study at Yale University found that 7 percent of American adults experience "mild levels of climate change psychological distress (CCPD)," and 3 percent suffer from "potentially serious levels of anxiety due to climate change."[39]

Years of studying precursors to radicalization tells me it's no coincidence that in 2023, the US surgeon general, Vivek

Murthy, declared the country to be suffering from an "epidemic of loneliness and isolation."[40] Half of Americans were telling pollsters they were lonely even before Covid-19, he reports—though he didn't recognize loneliness as a public health concern until 2014, when he served in the same position.[41] Concurrently, the adolescent depression rate nearly doubled between 2009 and 2019.[42] Why form relationships, get married, have kids, develop friendships, or do any of the things that give happiness and meaning to life if we're all going to die anyway?

There is absolutely no evidence warranting the explosive growth of conditions like "climate anxiety" and "eco-grief" as legitimate mental-health diagnoses. That's not science. That's a tool of mind control.

The Durability and Usefulness of Forced Phobias

When the world doesn't end on the prophesied day, why don't the followers of doomsday cults abandon their beliefs? When a self-proclaimed messiah is found to be a charlatan, a con man, or a perverted sex criminal (a common characteristic of cult leaders), why don't all people led into this delusion revolt and return to their normal lives?

As Carl Jung wrote in "After the Catastrophe," "The essence

of hysteria is a systematic dissociation."[43] Phobias and hysteria are closely linked. If you can get people to be irrationally terrified of something, they'll become increasingly detached from their own identity and the observable world around them. As this feeling grows over time, they will lapse into bouts of hysteria.

This is why victims of forced phobia seem so impervious to new facts or realities. Their fundamental sense of self has been under attack from the constant firing of synapses in their brain's fear center. And this traumatic rewiring of the mind creates openings for other mental weaknesses. Victims of "phobia indoctrination" are so far along in their dissociation that they can shrug off any contradictory or competing evidence.

When Gustave Le Bon wrote *The Crowd: A Study of the Popular Mind*, he asserted that when mobilized around a powerful fear or idea, individuals—but especially crowds—are capable of believing two things that should negate each other:

> The most contradictory ideas may be seen to be simultaneously current in crowds. According to the chances of the moment, a crowd will come under the influence of one of the various ideas stored up in its understanding, and is capable, in consequence, of committing the most dissimilar acts. Its complete lack of the critical spirit does not allow of its perceiving these contradictions.[44]

When Al Gore and John Kerry—America's high priests of the climate change movement—travel on private jets to conferences in Switzerland meant to address global warming, they're rightly criticized as hypocritical. But true believers of the climate movement always concoct a ready-made excuse, such as that the cause is more important than any individual's cost to the climate.

Additionally, those whose minds have been hijacked by politicized phobia discount contradictory evidence. This is why "stop oil" lunatics who superglue themselves to priceless works of art and form human blockades of public highways have trained themselves to deny reality. You cannot convince these people that their cause is absurd or that their tactics are counterproductive. For them, adherence to the cause is its own goal. They have a deep psychological need to prove that devotion. Their delusion is self-justifying.

Eric Hoffer addressed this in his seminal work on political psychology, *The True Believer*:

All active mass movements strive, therefore, to interpose a fact-proof screen between the faithful and the realities of the world. They do this by claiming that the ultimate and absolute truth is already embodied in their doctrine and that there is no truth nor certitude outside it. The facts on which the true believer bases his conclusions must not be derived from his experience of observation but from holy writ.[45]

Whether we are talking about climate cultists or any other group of zealots, resistance to change can be a formidable mental hurdle. Nobody wants to be wrong, especially on an issue of such magnitude as an "existential threat" to the human species. There is the emotional investment in the issue that often clouds rational thought. Group identity is also tied into shared belief, so the thought of abandoning such shared belief comes with the additional cost of losing connection to one's tribe. And for many people, that may be their greatest motivation.

To be separated from those around us—psychologically as much as physically—can leave us deeply unmoored. Human beings are not meant to be solitary. We need stimulation from our environment, and each other.

Taking that away can be a powerful tool to break down the mind. Totalitarians know this and exploit it to the fullest. If you make someone feel truly alone, they begin to collapse.

That's the power of isolation.

6

Isolation

Afghanistan, 2010

As I soared thousands of feet above the ground over eastern
Afghanistan in the summer of 2010, the war against the Taliban felt far away. I was flying on a UH-60 Black Hawk helicopter with senior military officers from Kabul to a border
region to meet with a special-operations element conducting
some of the most important strikes against high-value enemy
al-Qaeda targets.

I was struck by the natural beauty of the Afghan landscape.
The Kabul and Kunar Rivers met below and led into a flat,
large green plateau. But to the north, the jagged peaks of the
Hindu Kush mountains rocketed up out of the ground. It re-
minded me of backdrops from the *Lord of the Rings* movies. I
could see only occasional structures on the plateau below and
worked to tamp down my nagging unease: What if one of those

1980s Stinger missiles from the mujahideen era still somehow worked, and the bad guys in this area just happened to have one? Occasionally I'd spot settlements below. From thousands of feet up, they all looked the same: mudbrick walled compounds, out in the middle of nowhere. In most of them, you'd find villagers of the Pashtun ethnicity, doing what they could to scrape out a living in a rugged, impoverished country. We couldn't tell which ones from the air, but we knew that inside some of the compounds were Taliban fighters, with Kalashnikov rifles stacked up alongside some rocket-propelled grenades.

The Afghan government's control, based in Kabul in eastern Afghanistan along the border with Pakistan, was minimal. Maps show a major international border between Afghanistan and Pakistan, though practically speaking the border was a fiction. Illicit traffic of all kinds—particularly of Taliban fighters, weapons, and opium—transited back and forth constantly. The British in the nineteenth century called this the North-West Frontier Province, but that didn't change centuries of Pashtun tribal allegiances that ignored the lines drawn on maps.[1]

When I traveled outside of the major Afghan cities—which were dirty, chaotic, and tinged with the aerosolized soot of trash-burn pits—I could see vast swaths of countryside seemingly untouched by civilization. The dusky-brown walled compounds had neither running water nor electricity. Most of the

Afghan population lived in these primitive circumstances, which hadn't changed much over the course of millennia.

The imposition of the ubiquitous pale-blue burqa—a head-to-toe Islamic covering mandated for women in the Taliban era—was a visible reminder of how extremism can flourish in a corner of the world where Western influences were effectively eradicated. I still remember watching burqa-clad women trudging around the streets in Kabul and thinking, *How can this barbarism be possible in the twenty-first century?*

Largely because of its landlocked, rugged geography, Afghanistan is defined by isolation. It's almost impossible to exert central control over a country with so many geographic challenges and so little infrastructure. This also means that whoever is in charge (as we know, the Taliban easily retook control after President Biden's 2021 withdrawal) can wield tremendous influence over the population, with minimal interference from the outside world.

Throughout history, conquerors from Alexander the Great to the Mongols to the Soviets—and most recently US Operation Enduring Freedom—have learned the hard way the challenges of trying to pacify this area.[2] Mountain peoples, from the Scottish to the Kurds in Iraq to the Hmong in Vietnam, tend to resist central authority and are stubborn opponents of government control. Even Americans in Appalachia fit this profile.

In war-ravaged post-Soviet Afghanistan, the Taliban realized that isolation creates extreme psychological vulnerability—and they took advantage. It was the perfect place to create extremists—people isolated from other cultures and beliefs that conflict with the prescribed orthodoxy.

The Hermit Kingdom

Isolation as a tool of mind control can be enabled in many ways. It can come physically, as in the case of the mountains of Afghanistan. Or it can be imposed politically, as in North Korea, separated from the south by an arbitrary line on a map and cut off from the global internet by decree. Generally this is done under the aegis of protecting the people from "counterrevolutionary" forces. From Venezuela to Russia to China, repressive regimes isolate their populations from Western influence.

Why is isolation a powerful mind-control tactic? First, it creates anxiety and even fear, which we saw in the previous chapter is fertile ground for mass delusion. The idea that isolation can cause panic is firmly rooted in science. At the time of Chinese brainwashing's ascent in the 1950s, there were reports that extreme isolation through solitary confinement was a critical stage in the brainwashing process.[3]

The US and Canadian defense departments conducted their own experiments to see what would happen to individuals who experienced severe isolation. At McGill University, in one notorious example, students were placed in soundproof cubicles with a bare minimum of sight, sound, even touch—and no human contact. They had hoped to isolate these students in this manner for weeks to see what would happen. A handful made it a couple days. Most lasted only a few hours. What shocked researchers was the speed of mental decline. The subjects became anxious within minutes. Within hours, they were in panic, and then quickly slid into hallucinations. The scientists had to abandon the program.

Isolation is a powerful tool. It can break down the mind's defenses rapidly and cause intense physiological reactions. But isolation isn't simply a lack of external stimuli. People can feel isolated even in a crowd when they have no connection to their surroundings, their family members, or their past. That's why repressive regimes erase all ties to the past. It's why they attack religion—to separate the people from a relationship with God. And it's why they encourage the destruction of family bonds, to undermine the most important human relationships we have.

No nation is completely isolated from external influences, but North Korea comes closer than any other.

Even before the modern era, the Korean Peninsula was called "the Hermit Kingdom,"[4] because it was extremely hostile to outsiders. After Japan's defeat in 1945 and the Korean Peninsula's subsequent division between the Soviets and the United

States, North Korea's Communist leader took its hermit status to a whole new level.

With the exception of high party officials, North Koreans rarely have passports or the ability to visit other countries. They have no access to the regular global internet, and any connection to their national intranet is tightly monitored by censors who check in every five minutes.[5] *Wired* reported in 2023 that cell phones had proliferated among the population (more than half of adults had them), but their connection speeds were so slow and their content so heavily monitored that only the most basic functions were possible.[6] Caught with unapproved Western literature in North Korea? Execution. Found with a Bible? Execution again. Teens watching South Korean videos? Twelve years of hard labor.

For the twenty-six million inhabitants of North Korea, there is deep, inescapable isolation from everything.

It's this mass isolation, along with the omnipresent threat of imprisonment and execution for even the most minor offenses, that has allowed the bizarre cult of personality known as the Kim dynasty to rule as absolute tyrants in their corner of the world.

Kim Jong Un is the closest thing today to a pure despot. He is the third Kim to run the "Democratic People's Republic of North Korea," which the Soviet-trained Kim Il Sung established in 1948. He passed power to his son Kim Jong Il, and upon his death in 2011, Kim Jong Un inherited it. It should be noted that despite the line of succession, Kim Il Sung is still considered the "eternal" president of the DPRK, which led the writer Christopher Hitchens, after a visit in 2001, to suggest describing the nation as a "necrocracy"[7] (rule by the dead).

North Korea copies the past isolation tactics of Japan, its former occupier, which, at one point in its history, shut itself off to the West for two centuries while worshipping its emperor as a direct descendant of the divine. North Korea went further, building on this old Japanese model with the addition of cultish traits more evocative of New Age religions.

It's common to see massive crowds of North Koreans bawling on command for state television cameras, shedding tears of gratitude and awe for their "Supreme Leader," Kim Jong Un. They believe he, his father, and his grandfather selflessly suffer for them, are too perfect to urinate or defecate,[8] and that North Korea found the cure for AIDS and created the hamburger.[9] And the ones who don't really believe this are careful enough to act like they do.

Hitchens wondered in such an isolated and psychologically disturbed nation "whether mass delusion is the only thing that keeps a people sane," as his essay's subhead put it.[10] It's a question that I have considered many times in the context of North Korea, a land where the tactics of mind control have been taken to extremes at almost every level. Their people are forced into such extreme delusions, it's hard for outsiders to believe it's possible for a mind to see the world in that way.

Of course, the Kim dynasty engages in all forms of mind control—conditioning, menticide, reeducation, and more—to force the population into delusional compliance. Portraits of the "Great Leader" (Kim Il Sung) and the "Dear Leader" (Kim Jong Il) are required to be prominently displayed in every home, and any damage to these portraits is a criminal offense. The entire reality of North Korea is as though a regime of psychopaths were treating Orwell's *1984* as a how-to manual. But isolation from the outside world remains the critical tactic to keep the system together. The removal of any outside influence keeps the brainwashed masses untainted by reality.

North Korea also isolates its citizens from one another by turning neighbor against neighbor. Individuals become psychologically distanced from their own family members as the state warns that they cannot be trusted. Mass psychosis runs so deep in North Korea that it often penetrates even the relationship between mother and child.

In 2023, I interviewed North Korean defector Yeonmi Park on my podcast. She said things so horrifying about the regime's treatment of her and her family that I found myself going back to the show transcript afterward to make sure that I had heard it correctly. On the level of fear (forced phobia, of course, is another mind-control tactic North Korea has mastered), Yeonmi told me:

> I still remember the very first thing that my mom told me as a young girl was that don't even whisper because the birds and mice could hear me. If I said the one thing that was wrong, they were not going to execute me. They were going to execute three to eight generations of my family. After this kind of dark era I decided to escape from my homeland when I was thirteen years old.[11]

Imagine the psychological trauma of that conversation alone. A mother tells her daughter that there are ears listening everywhere, she lives in an all-knowing surveillance state, and if she says the wrong thing about the Kim regime, this child will condemn herself, and multiple generations of her bloodline, to execution. It's an unthinkable burden apparently intended to commit menticide on a child at the earliest possible stage. It also creates a dynamic of extreme loneliness: If a child cannot speak freely to her parents, or wonder aloud, that child becomes a prisoner of her own mind.

As for the isolation of the North Korean people overall, here is how Yeonmi described her escape from the mass concentration camp of North Korea en route to Mongolia:

The survival rate of that desert is not even 1 percent. We had to walk in the -40 degrees in the winter in 2009. So they literally just gave us a compass and said, "Go walk across a north and west direction and cross eight wire fences. And if you don't die from the cold or the wild animals and the border guards, if you find Mongolian soldiers, tell them that you want to go to South Korea." We did that. Luckily, we didn't die from all those things and got to Mongolia. And then, of course, the soldiers, the first thing they were telling us was that they want to send us back to China and go back to North Korea by sending North Koreans back to their countries, like catching a Jew and sending them to Auschwitz. We are going to be facing execution, torture, unimaginable things that are happening against humanity.[12]

In the context of North Korea, those lucky enough to defect successfully (countless others fail and are executed) had to confront the world of delusions they had been forced to live in. This itself was a painstaking process, as the only life they had ever known was built by lies atop a mountain of other lies.

The type of isolation imposed on North Koreans is extreme. But there is also a kind of isolation experienced by those exiled from a life they had once known, often through warfare or other disasters that cause mass migration. I saw with my own eyes how the desire to end such isolation can be strong enough to overcome the fear even of death.

War's Evil Wager: Isolation or Your Life?

Syria–Jordan Border, 2013

Nobody wanted to be at Zaatari, but over 120,000 people were. A Syrian refugee camp about five miles inside Jordan, Zaatari was a sweltering sprawl of tents and hastily built structures—a desert city of lamentations. When I was there in 2013, it was the fourth-largest city in Jordan. The nearby Syrian civil war was at a boiling point, and more than a million civilians had fled.[13]

When I recall crouching in those tents, I can still feel their oppressive heat. Families of five or six were crammed together under simple canvas awnings, with little more than thin sleeping rolls and a tea set, no air-conditioning, no running water. Some families were luckier, living inside trailers with more basic comforts at hand.

Going in, I was prepared for a refugee camp to be a place of sorrow and pain. But the stories I heard in them, I can never forget. Accompanied by a good friend of mine from the US, a Circassian-Jordanian who translated Arabic for me, I met with a Syrian father who had witnessed an entire family in his neighborhood machine-gunned to death. Their offense? They had water bottles that members of the *shabiha*, the Syrian dictator Bashar al-Assad's thug militia, believed had come from Zaatari. The *shabiha* goons claimed anyone who was crossing the border back and forth into Syria was a spy, and they opened fire on them. Not even small children were spared.

While I had been in war zones before, my time in Iraq and Afghanistan was spent with intelligence officers and warfighters. The immediacy of fighting bad guys allowed me to focus on the mission. Broader philosophical questions—What exactly were we trying to accomplish in either of those wars? Was my contribution to that effort meaningful at all?—could wait until I got home to the States.

But in the Zaatari camp, there was no escape from the pain of war all around. Being so close to deeply traumatized people who have faced evil in its purest form is difficult to process. Their voices, their faces—there was an exhausted agony to them. Walking down the dusty dirt roads of the camp site, I was just another powerless Western civilian hoping to tell the stories of evil that Assad had committed without exploiting a ravaged people for clicks and clout.

The Syrian children were curious about me. A few asked if I wanted to take a photo with them (which, after getting Mom and Dad's permission, I did). Many of the adults were wary, even distrustful. Given what they had been through, that made sense. How could you trust anyone when your own countrymen had turned your native land into a cauldron of carnage?

Though surrounded by more than 120,000 fellow Syrians in close quarters, these refugees still felt alone. Humanitarian relief organizations gave them food and medical care, but these Syrians felt forgotten. Separated from everything they'd known, and now deeply uncertain about their futures, the refugees of Zaatari lived in an isolation that went far beyond geographic circumstances.

Human beings are social creatures. As a species, we have brains that are hardwired to thrive through contact with, first and foremost, our families, as they're the most familiar to us and important to our survival. Then there are a whole range of groupings—community, tribe, religious sect, nation—to which we feel additional allegiance and belonging. Strip that away, and we begin to feel unmoored, anxious, even fearful.

I didn't detect any radicalism in Zaatari camp. But it's easy to see how distrust, hatred, and bloodlust could spread like wildfire in a place of such desperate and lonely people.

And yet I kept hearing a common refrain among the refugees of Zaatari: They wanted to return home to Syria. Despite everything they'd been through—the violence, atrocities, and displacement—they still dreamed of returning to their villages. If their villages no longer existed, they wanted to rebuild them.

Maybe this was mostly their reaction to life in a refugee camp. But fathers like the one I spoke with—who saw an entire family killed over water bottles—were nonetheless planning to return.

The pain of the war was palpable. But the pain of isolation—of being estranged from your country, your home, and your countrymen forever—was worse. And the refugees I spoke to at Zaatari were willing to walk back to hell to end that isolation.

Ultimately, isolation created an opening for evil, but it also fed a yearning for restoration. When I left the camp, I was uncertain which would win.

The Punishment of Ostracism

Separation from the community can be a punishment as effective as locking people in cells or cages. In ancient Athens, the practice of ostracism began in the fifth century BC. Named for the ostracon, shards of clay pottery on which the votes were cast, ostracism was essentially a vote to banish a public figure for ten years.[14] If the man (it was always a man) attempted to return before the end of his decade-long banishment, he would be executed. This practice was sometimes used to prevent well-established Athenian citizens from gaining too much power and becoming tyrants. Themistocles, the great hero of the Athenians' naval victory at Salamis in 480 BC against a massive Persian invasion, was himself ostracized.

But behind ostracism was a straightforward notion: To be separated from the community limits one's power and, in most cases, is an effective form of punishment. Connection to community is important for all of us and has been throughout history. Jews enforced synagogue bans from Talmudic times; Catholicism's legacy of excommunication dates back to the earliest days of the church. We still punish certain lesser criminals with house arrest.

Ostracism limits power but it also has the potential to break the mind. In the Soviet gulag system of the twentieth century, prisoners were separated not just from their families and friends but the civilization they had known altogether. Tens of millions were sent to freezing prison camps in remote areas like Siberia and northern Russia, and millions of them died there. In the Vietnam War, the North Vietnamese held American prisoners of war in "tiger cages" meant for a single individual, separating them from fellow American soldiers and subjecting them to atrociously inhumane conditions.

The physical conditions of forced isolation are often intentionally depraved. Everyone has seen in movies where prisoners in dank, dark cells are slowly rotting with heavy chains affixed to their limbs and rats scurrying over their bodies. But the psychological torture of isolation was always intentional. The body can adapt to discomfort and even pain. Mental anguish is inescapable.

Starting around the thirteenth century in Europe, castles in

England and France had a dungeon called an "oubliette" (from the French verb *oublier*, "to forget"). This grim prison was simply a hole in the stone floor of the castle leading to a vertical passageway and a tiny cell at the bottom so narrow that the prisoner couldn't lie down. Once the prisoner had been thrown into the oubliette, a steel grate was bolted shut over the top of the entry hole, and the prisoner was left to slowly die in both physical and psychological agony.

While incarcerated, our minds are left to ruminate on a range of possibilities. Will we be tortured? Executed? Will we ever see loved ones again? Will they ever know what happened to us? The moment we are taken captive and separated from the outside world, our minds begin to break down. An isolated person is a weakened one. All the worst dictators in history knew this—and capitalized on it. Modern cult leaders have done the same. Finding those who are physically or emotionally disconnected from their fellow human beings is always an opportunity for totalitarian belief.

Cults and Family Separation

If you've ever been to a corporate retreat and some of your colleagues became a little too enthusiastic about the company line—you might have told them, mockingly, "Don't drink the Kool-Aid."

Unfortunately, this phrase comes from a cult atrocity—specifically, the Jonestown massacre of 1978. Over nine hundred people died in this mass self-poisoning event, including more than two hundred children, many of whom were killed by their own parents.[15] Jim Jones, the cult leader of the Peoples Temple, ordered his followers to drink cyanide-laced Flavor Aid (not Kool-Aid), and almost everyone obeyed.

How did this atrocity happen? Jim Jones used many totalitarian brainwashing tactics we have laid out so far—but isolating members physically and socially was central to his plan. In *Collective Illusions*, developmental psychologist and author Todd Rose wrote of Jim Jones that "even before isolating them in a deep jungle, he demanded that they sacrifice their possessions, their homes, and even, in some cases, custody of their children to his cause. Once in Jonestown, members had their passports and medications taken away from them, and all their communications with the outside world were censored."[16]

Once the Peoples Temple members were isolated, Jim Jones's power over them grew dramatically. That's why he wanted to move them to Guyana in the 1970s—a desperately poor country generally outside the reach of US law enforcement. When his cult members were in the middle of the jungle, Jones could use his armed goons to surveil their every move and threaten them into compliance. Removing contact with the outside world also made it easier for him to maintain the loyalty of the brainwashed true believers in his midst. Plus, it was known that Jones encouraged family members to inform on each other if their belief or commitment to his pseudo-religious Communist cause wavered.

Pitting family members against one another is a form of weaponized isolation common in cults. Take Scientology, which achieved tax-exempt status in the US as a religious organization in 1993—despite the fact that normal people understand that it's a cult. "In the 21st century, everyone has a right to believe in anything or nothing. But not everything that claims to be a religion is a religion. It could be, for example, a brain washing cult,"[17] reasons BBC reporter and Scientology critic John Sweeney, whose book on it is aptly titled *The Church of Fear*.

Scientology admits to pressuring members to "disconnect" from relatives or friends who leave Scientology, because lapsed Scientologists are supposedly "suppressive." This threat of isolation is often enough to keep most Scientologists locked into the cult for life.

Expulsion from Scientology can be triggered by criminal acts, its website says, or

through the commitment of acts deemed Suppressive Acts in the Scientology Justice Codes—which includes the Suppressive Act of publicly renouncing the faith, an act which in Scientology, as well as almost every religion, is grounds for automatic expulsion.

When someone has been expelled from the religion, that person loses both his or her fellowship with the Church as well as with other Scientologists. The condition lasts until they have been restored to good standing.[18]

It seems extreme, but Scientology is merely imposing a modern form of ancient Athenian ostracism. More often than not, that threat is enough to keep the delusion of their cult members alive.

Isolation is critical to the formation of cults. The NXIVM cult started out in 1998 as a multilevel marketing scheme. By the time the Justice Department began its investigation in 2017, NXIVM had become a messianic quasi-religion, with its founder, Keith Raniere (now serving a 120-year prison sentence), running a sex-trafficking operation catering to his own sadistic desires.[19] As so many cults do, Raniere's had its own bizarre rituals and rules (including the heinous practice of branding some women). But isolating his victims from the world around them was a central goal from the start. In the opening weeks of Executive Success Programs (the gateway offering to NXIVM cult), prospects would be subjected to seventeen-hour-long indoctrination barrages, meant to break them down with fatigue and to cut off their contact with outside influences.[20]

Every exploitative, destructive cult demands isolation. Their theological or self-help beliefs can vary dramatically—some are built around a self-professed messiah, others are focused on the apocalypse—but the process they use to manipulate followers is eerily similar.

Atomization: Isolation Within Society

Cults seek to separate members—who often already feel isolated to begin with—from their families and the rest of society. Weak egos, emotional vulnerability, dissociative propensities, and "tenuous, deteriorated, or nonexistent family relations and support systems" all increase people's susceptibility and recruitment, experts believe.[21]

Totalitarian governments operate in many ways like a massive cult. In *The Origins of Totalitarianism*, Hannah Arendt introduced the concept of "social atomization," which, coupled with "communal disintegration," is the precondition for an absolutist state.[22] Arendt made the case that atomization was the basis of totalitarian rule. Without an atomized population, you couldn't enforce the contradictory, arbitrary orthodoxies of a totalitarian state. She wrote that "[t]he evidence of Hitler's as well as Stalin's dictatorship points clearly to the fact that isolation of atomized individuals provides not only the mass basis for totalitarian rule, but is carried through to the very top of the whole structure."[23]

According to Arendt, someone who is atomized is lonely, is

disconnected from normal social relationships, lacks self-esteem, and is looking for someone to provide answers. The dictator demagogue then swoops in and offers connection, solidarity, and purpose to the "mass man" (a person whose isolation makes totalitarian mobilization possible). As Arendt describes it, "the masses grew out of the fragments of a highly atomized society whose competitive structure and concomitant loneliness of the individual had been held in check only through membership in a class. The chief characteristic of the mass man is not brutality and backwardness, but his isolation and lack of normal social relationships."[24]

This form of isolation is all about psychology instead of proximity. A person can be living in the midst of a bustling city, going to work every day, and return home feeling deeply atomized.

In order to "protect" atomized people, the state centralizes power and monopolizes force, which prevents the frictions within a society from breaking it apart. But in doing so, the state creates the need for an overarching ideology (nationalism in the case of Nazi Germany, Communism in Soviet Russia) that will hold everything together and create a justification mythology for the excesses of the state.[25] The ideology replaces all the former modes of meaning and relationship that would have kept atomization at bay. Thus, as the state becomes more atomized, it becomes more ideological, again making it more atomized.

Dictatorships in the twentieth century all took this similar path to atomization. Hitler, Stalin, Mao, and Pol Pot enacted systematic efforts to break the people away from their previous sense of identity and shared history. Once this step had taken place, there was disconnection and fear (forced phobia) within the society, which allowed the new political masters to, as Arendt put it, "rationalize the essentially futile feelings of self-importance and hysterical security that it offered to the isolated individuals of an atomized society."[26] Those who have been indoctrinated with fear will quickly latch onto any philosophy—no matter how absurd or vulgar—that puffs up their ego and promises them security.

When Robert Jay Lifton wrote about the process of Maoist reeducation in *Thought Reform and the Psychology of Totalism*, one of the mechanisms of psychological isolation he identified was intentionally crowded prison cells—seemingly the opposite of isolation. But in fact, the initial phase of a prisoner's reeducation was psychologically isolating him within a crowd. The prisoner didn't enter a community that could help him retain his identity. Instead, he was bombarded by a barrage of groupthink and made to feel deeply alone.

According to Lifton, a prisoner would be "placed in a small (8' x 12') bare cell which already contained eight other prisoners, all of them Chinese"[27] and all of them further along in their own reeducation processes, eager to earn praise from their captors. Their role was to pressure and isolate the new detainee from the world he had known before incarceration.

Once inside the cell, Lifton writes, the "'cell chief' identified himself, and addressing [the subject] by his newly-acquired prison number, instructed him to sit in the center of the cell while the other prisoners formed a circle around him."[28] This circle of prisoners would then take turns shouting at the newly arrived prisoner, "denouncing him as an 'imperialist' and a 'spy,' and demanding that he 'recognize' his crimes and 'confess everything' to the 'government.'"[29]

In this way, the "thought reform" jailers of China could subject a prisoner to constant human presence, and this would only bolster their feelings of isolation—from the world, reality, and life he had previously known.

What happened in the jail cell, the Chinese also pushed on a national scale. When Chairman Mao began his Cultural Revolution in 1966, he destroyed Chinese identity by demanding a struggle against the "Four Olds": old things, ideas, customs, and habits. He dispatched urban youths to root out—with violence, even against the elderly—anything bourgeois or traditional. Five years later, longtime *New York Times* correspondent Tillman Durdin reported from Hong Kong on a transformed landscape:

In not a single home seen by the writer was there any family altar, any tablets to ancestors or any representation of the old gods formerly worshipped by the Chinese masses. . . . No religious practices were discoverable during the trip in China, and guides said there were none. Religious edifices have been turned to use as schools, warehouses or recreational centers. . . . No traditional operas, no traditional music and no traditional plays are performed these days. There are only the 10 new standard dramatic works developed during the Cultural Revolution and performed everywhere now in full or in excerpts.[30]

Old China was being murdered, and with it anyone's sense of being Chinese outside of Mao and the Party. Like the torture so often used in brainwashing, isolation created a blank slate for Mao to impose his sadistic ideals.

Americans feel increasingly isolated, but not because of dictatorship or a sprawling system of political prisons. It's because our culture is rapidly shifting as forces on the Left work to tear down and wipe away our history.

I remember in July 2020 there was a small army of police officers gathered at the Columbus Circle monument in New York City, at the southwest corner of Central Park. It wasn't one or two cops—it was more like fifty of them, with quick-reaction vehicles parked nearby. I asked one of the officers why they were all standing guard. It wasn't, he told me, because they were worried about another BLM march passing through and disrupting traffic, as had been the threat for much of that summer.

The cops were there to defend the statue of Columbus itself from the American-flag-burning mob organized by BLM's ally, the Revolutionary Communist Party, USA.

I lived just a few blocks from Columbus Circle at the time and had never paid much notice to the statue, which was my mistake. It's impressive. A massive bronze Christopher Columbus stands atop a column above representations of the three boats he used to cross the Atlantic in 1492. Designed by the Italian sculptor Gaetano Russo, it was dedicated in 1892 as a symbol of Italian American pride.[31]

I thought about what was going on as I walked away from the monument and weighed the mob's arguments for canceling Columbus against the fact that this explorer brought continents together and changed the world forever. Thanks to his bravery, the old and new worlds—both fallible—were introduced to each other. We know what happens when civilizations meet for the first time, and Columbus's arrival must be taken in the context of fifteenth-century morality—not twenty-first.

Many Italian Americans are proud of the Genoa-born sailor, and most Americans accept him as an important figure in their national history. But isolating people from their shared history is a valuable tactic of totalitarian mass movements.

"It is obvious that a proselytizing mass movement must break down all existing ties if it is to win a considerable following. The ideal potential convert is the individual who stands alone, who has no collective body he can blend with and lose himself in and so mask the pettiness, meaninglessness and shabbiness of his individual existence," writes Eric Hoffer in *The True Believer*.[32]

Today, the Left assaults the "Western-prescribed nuclear family structure" (as condemned by the Black Lives Matter movement).[33] It tears down statues and monuments—whether ones erected for Confederates in the South or ones erected for otherwise great men who owned slaves in the North. Not even Abraham Lincoln is safe: San Francisco's school board voted in 2021 to erase his name from its buildings for his role in quelling an 1862 Native American uprising. Naturally George Washington—a slave owner—was also erased in this righteous reckoning.

One of the most insidious isolation tactics employed by the Left in recent years is the "1619 Project," a journalism-series-turned-educational-curriculum initiated by *The New York Times* in 2019. Its revisionist thesis is that America's true founding wasn't in 1776, when we declared independence and began what has become the longest-running constitutional democracy in the world. Rather, we were founded in 1619, when more than twenty enslaved Africans arrived in Virginia. Everything we are as a nation is a function of black slavery and white supremacy. That's supposed to be our new foundational belief.

In the *Times'* own words, the project "aims to reframe the country's history by placing the consequences of slavery and the contributions of black Americans at the very center of our national narrative."[34] Time to erase the old heroes, old beliefs, old ideals, old everything (Mao would be proud).

What is the effect of this effort to disconnect us from our past? We become isolated, anxious, and fearful. We lose our shared touch points. We relinquish many of the mental and emotional bonds that hold us together over the vast expanse of this nation. We are atomized and longing for new meaning to replace what's been taken from us.

And what often comes next? The exploitation of this emptiness through identity construction.

7

Identity Construction

Manhattan, 2016

Five years had passed since I left the CIA and the NYPD Intelligence Division for a media career. But once you've heard a bomb go off, you never forget the sound.

I was mixing a drink for friends at a gathering on my Manhattan rooftop when we all heard the explosion. It was eight thirty on a warm Saturday night in September 2016. Maybe it was a car backfiring or firecracker, my guests theorized. But I knew instinctively what it was, right in my Chelsea neighborhood. There was commotion around me as we went to see what had happened. We all started pacing and wondering what would be next.

My role in the world had changed. I was a civilian now, and as a national security commentator for *The Blaze* I used my counterterrorism expertise to make sense of things like this for viewers.

Calling 911 was unnecessary; I could already hear a small army of NYPD and first responders racing up Sixth Avenue. Although I was physically close to the explosion, I felt far away from my old desk inside the Intelligence Division. Some years before, I would have been working with the FBI Joint Terrorism Task Forces to try to figure out who did this.

I still had the numbers of people I had worked with at the NYPD, so I called someone at the Intelligence Division to ask what was going on. Were there additional threats I needed to be aware of? I reached him as he was on the way out the door—he had been called into the office because of the explosion and at that point didn't know any more about it than I did.

But before he hung up, he offered one piece of intel he could share: Earlier that day, authorities had discovered several pipe bombs planted along the route of a US Marine Corps charity 5K race in New Jersey. One exploded but thankfully didn't injure anyone. That something had just gone off—a few hundred yards from my apartment building—was too coincidental. There was a terrorist on the loose, and the people of New York City were in danger.

Indeed, thirty-one people were wounded by the homemade pressure cooker bomb that exploded on West Twenty-Third

Street that night. One woman had to be rushed to the emergency room after ball-bearing projectiles pierced her abdomen and wood pieces lodged in her neck.[1] In a technique I'd seen countless times deployed overseas, the bomber had wrapped the device in ball bearings to increase the lethality of the explosion with extra shrapnel.

Fortunately, no one was killed. According to *The New York Times*, the explosion was "powerful enough to vault a heavy steel Dumpster more than 120 feet through the air. . . . Windows shattered 400 feet from where the explosion went off, and pieces of the bomb were recovered 650 feet away."[2]

An unexploded bomb was also found on West Twenty-Seventh Street. A total of ten devices were found in the New York area.[3] A few days later, during his capture and arrest in New Jersey, the bomber shot multiple police officers.

Eventually we learned the perpetrator was Ahmad Khan Rahami—and he followed the homegrown terrorist script I was all too familiar with. During my time with the NYPD Intelligence Division, the jihadist group we were most concerned was plotting attacks on the homeland was called AQAP (al-Qaeda in the Arabian Peninsula). AQAP's former leader, Anwar al-Awlaki, was American born. He was one of the Americans killed by a drone strike authorized by President Barack Obama in Yemen in 2011. Rahami read AQAP's online magazine *Inspire*, which included articles such as "Make a Bomb in the Kitchen of Your Mom," and a step-by-step guide to building improvised explosives, like the Chelsea pressure-cooker device.[4]

Born in Afghanistan, Rahami was a self-radicalized jihadist who claimed to be inspired by Osama bin Laden.[5] His own father had called the FBI on him because he was worried that his son had become a terrorist.[6] The FBI had met with the elder Rahami, done some cursory background checks on the younger—and that was it. Though Rahami had been on their radar for years, the FBI couldn't act because he wasn't breaking any laws—until he did.

Rahami's profile was similar to those of other jihadist terrorists, including those responsible for far more lethal attacks. The Tsarnaev brothers—who used pressure-cooker bombs to kill and maim Boston Marathon participants and spectators in 2013—were devoted readers of *Inspire* magazine.[7] Also indoctrinated through *Inspire*: Omar Mateen, who killed forty-nine people at the Pulse nightclub in Orlando, and Syed Farook, the mass shooter in San Bernardino, California, who killed fourteen.[8]

The purpose of materials like *Inspire* is to convert more jihadis. The ultimate goal is reshaping the identity of its readers so that they will see themselves as one and the same with al-Qaeda's mission. This process is called identity construction.

Lose Yourself in the Madness

Weeks before I returned to New York City in 2009, the NYPD Intelligence Division and FBI Joint Terrorism Task Force arrested an Afghan immigrant named Najibullah Zazi—another self-radicalized jihadist with al-Qaeda ties. He was a legal permanent US resident living in Denver and was planning an attack on New York City that would have been the worst since 9/11 had the FBI not disrupted it in time.

Zazi had trained in explosives at a terrorist facility in Pakistan and was plotting with co-conspirators to conduct suicide bombings in the New York City subway at the busiest possible locations and times of day. Zazi had both the ideological commitment and wherewithal to pull off these mass-casualty suicide attacks.

For months after his capture, we had debriefings in the office about his case and tried to apply lessons learned so the FBI and NYPD could stop future attacks. My proximity to the Zazi case was a constant reminder that our mass transit system was a very real vulnerability.

As a native New Yorker, I had a handle on the teeming mass of disordered humanity in the subway system. But, sitting in the Intel Division office scouring operational files on Zazi, I was haunted by the specter of a transit attack that happened while I was still in high school—one that I, along with the rest of the world, forgot: the 1995 sarin gas attack on the Tokyo subway system by the Aum Shinrikyō cult, whose experiences with brainwashing we discussed in chapter 3.

The sarin attack killed eleven and injured five thousand. Experts believe to this day that if the sarin had been more expertly prepared and deployed, it could have killed a hundred thousand people or more. As Robert Jay Lifton describes the scene in *Destroying the World to Save It*:

> A male cult member boarded each of the trains carrying two or three small plastic bags covered with newspaper and, at an agreed-upon time, removed the newspaper and punctured the bags with a sharpened umbrella tip. . . . [P]eople coughed, choked, experienced convulsions, and collapsed.[9]

Why did Aum Shinrikyō members want to kill as many people as possible in a totally random attack in the Japanese subway system? Their leader, Shoko Asahara, believed that hastening the end of the world was doing humanity a favor. Aum Shinrikyō wanted to achieve, in Dr. Lifton's words, "purification and renewal of humankind through the total or near-total destruction of the planet."[10]

Aum Shinrikyō was a classic cult in terms of its indoctrination processes, which Lifton calls a "totalistic community" where "everything had to be experienced on an all-or-nothing basis."[11] In order to become a part of it, members had to express their total devotion and obedience—no half-measures. These acolytes were bombarded with cult indoctrination tactics. They were isolated from the outside world, their self-identity dissolved into the group. Nothing existed outside the cult. Like al-Qaeda-inspired jihadis, they were willing to take countless lives—including their own—to remain true to their delusional beliefs. How could anyone let this happen to themselves?

The answers can be found in the group psychology of identity construction.

Eric Hoffer, in *The True Believer*, writes:

> To ripen a person for self-sacrifice he must be stripped of his individual identity and distinctness. He must cease to be George, Hans, Ivan, or Tadao—a human atom with an existence bounded by birth and death. The most dramatic way to achieve this end is by the complete assimilation of the individual into the collective body. The fully assimilated individual does not see himself and others as human beings.[12]

Over the course of our lifetimes, we form our individual sense of self through a collection of identity markers built by experience, history, family, tradition, and place. No one person is born the same as anyone else, and no one has the same upbringing and environment—even identical twins have their own minute peculiarities. Thus, every person becomes distinct from the billions of other people who exist or have ever existed on earth.

But totalitarian regimes seek to replace our individual identity with the group's identity, creating, as Joost Meerloo says, "a society of robots, not men."[13] Human beings are to be programmed like computers, a procedure that requires sameness. Individuality is a complicating factor for totalitarian systems. Constructing an effective group identity therefore requires the eradication of uniqueness.

This is why cults and extreme religious sects often insist their members wear uniforms. Guru Bhagwan Shree Rajneesh's cult out in Oregon in the 1980s had its adherents wear bright orange and red robes, for example.[14] Hitler's street thugs wore brown (they were called "brownshirts") during their ascent to power, whereas Mussolini's Italian fascists of the same era wore black. Neo-Nazis are called "skinheads" because they shave their heads. The shock troops of left-wing street protests in the US and Europe are called "black bloc" because they dress in black clothing from head to toe.

Jihadists who are being radicalized while living in the United States generally grow out a long, unkempt beard— sometimes dyed red or orange with henna to honor the Prophet

Muhammad. They also tend to wear what we would consider traditional Middle Eastern dress, a long shirt-dress called a *thobe* in Saudi Arabia and elsewhere in the Arab world.

All of these style adoptions are physical manifestations of ideological hardening. They are external stimuli meant to impose inward conformity. Jihadists, cults, mobs, and totalitarians use identity construction as a tool of mental coercion when radicalizing members. Their mode of dress, hairstyles, and cultural choices all reflect—and shape—their new constructed identity.

Drawing on data from 217 federal terrorism cases, the US Department of Justice published a 2018 meta-analysis of terrorist psychology called "How Radicalization to Terrorism Occurs in the United States."[15] The researchers theorized that identity creation is central to the radicalization process. The *Diagnostic and Statistical Manual of Mental Disorders* (*DSM-5*), the core reference text for psychiatry, notes, "The key to understanding undue influence is the creation of a dual identity, which can result in dissociative identity disorder," formerly known as "multiple-personality disorder."

Someone with dissociative identity disorder may have two or more personality states in their head, and may switch between identities. The *DSM-5* describes the mind-control tactics that can give rise to dissociative identity disorder:

Individuals who have been subjected to intense coercive persuasion (e.g., brainwashing, thought reform, indoctrination while captive, torture, long-term political imprisonment, recruitment by sects/cults or by terror organizations) may present with prolonged changes in, or conscious questioning of, their identity.[16]

The DOJ report categorized identity according to salience and pervasiveness, and found that "if an identity is salient, it is more likely to be brought to bear in a particular situation. If an identity is pervasive, it is more likely to be brought to bear in numerous situations. . . . Individuals with more salient and pervasive terrorist identities would be more likely to engage in terrorism."[17]

For example, the report found that "individuals who attended more group meetings and had been group members for longer periods of time committed a larger number of terrorist incidents and were charged with more criminal counts."[18]

One key lever that enables this identity-construction process is guilt. Jihadist radicalizers like Anwar al-Awlaki, the Twenty-Third Street bomber's spiritual guru, would sermonize the deaths of children caused by Western wars in Muslim countries such as Iraq and Afghanistan. Awlaki's eulogies not only generated antipathy toward the United States and its allies but also stirred feelings of guilt in the Muslims listening. In Awlaki's telling, many Muslims stood by and did nothing while their coreligionists were murdered. The listener might have thought of himself as a moral man, a professional, and maybe even an American—but now, disgusted with his inaction, sheds that identity for a new one. (Notice the relation to forced phobia, where subjects are induced to fear others and fear their own failure to act. Guilt and fear are intertwined.)

Ultimately, weaponized guilt is meant to turn people's moral frameworks against them as a tool of control. Overwhelming guilt undermines confidence in their identity, clouds their overall cognition, and allows for the totalitarian belief system (spiritual or political) to build them anew. This remaking of identity can come through either self-radicalization from contact with text or videos or the more active radicalization that comes from an external force—be it a cult, religious extremist, or political figure.

Regardless, total surrender to guilt—followed by confession, as evidenced in brainwashing—is a clear sign that the construction of a new identity is now able to proceed without resistance. In Joost Meerloo's work on menticide, he describes this point as "the masochistic pact," which is "the last gift and trick the tortured gives to his torturer. It is as if he were to call out, 'Be good to me. I confess. I submit. Be good to me and love me.'

After having suffered all manner of brutality, hypnotism, despair, and panic, there is a final quest for human companionship, but it is ambivalent, mixed with deep despising, hatred, and bitterness."[19]

One of the ways identity switch can happen is through "Stockholm syndrome," when one identifies with one's captors. The term came from a famous 1973 bank robbery and hostage crisis in Sweden's capital city. Jan-Erik Olsson plotted to rob the Kreditbanken in Stockholm, take hostages, and in the process demand the release from prison of his associate, Clark Olofsson.[20] Olsson fired warning shots into the ceiling, took four bank employees into the vault, tied leashes on them, and began a long standoff with the police, who surrounded the bank. The Kreditbanken hostage situation would go on for six days.

The robbery became a global phenomenon. The negotiations even involved the prime minister of Sweden, Olof Palme. Olsson was successful in getting his pal Olofsson freed—and in an almost unthinkable police blunder, he was allowed to join Olsson inside the bank during the siege.[21]

Initially the hostages were willing to help the police; one of them held up fingers to show how many hostages were inside the bank.[22] But over time, that changed. Joel Dimsdale writes in *Dark Persuasion: A History of Brainwashing from Pavlov to Social Media* that one of the hostages "reported after her release: 'The robber told me that everything would be all right if only the police would go away. . . . Yes, I thought, it is the police who are keeping me from my children.'"[23] The hostages had come to believe that the police—not the hostage takers—were the real threat.

Another effective identity construction tactic—as discussed at length in the previous chapter—is preventing contact with the outside world. The military uses this (for good reason), limiting communication with anyone off base for a number of weeks. It helps speed up the transition from civilian to warrior. But, of course, this type of socialized isolation can be used to bad ends as well.

Robert Jay Lifton calls this isolation tactic "milieu control."[24] The word *milieu* means "environment" in French. More specifically, Dr. Lifton is referring to cults and totalitarian ideologies where "all communication, including even an individual's inner communication, is monopolized and orchestrated."[25] This extreme degree of control makes it possible to construct a new identity on a much faster timeline with fewer distractions or impediments. North Korea sends children to work camps for the crime of watching South Korean music videos for the same reason that cult leaders insist that phone calls home to one's family from the compound must stop. Those in power want to prevent or erase contradictory inputs into the mind and replace them with schematics of their own design.

Sometimes, the best way to accomplish identity construction isn't with a dictatorship's prison cells or a cult's threats of eternal damnation. Especially effective in the early stages of identity construction is a tactic called "love bombing." Love bombing is a mind-manipulation technique that brings much more insidious ends to the age-old practice of buttering someone up so you can take advantage of them. Jim Jones in the Peoples Temple was famous for making new recruits feel as if they were the center of his universe. For cults that often prey on the lonely and listless, "love bombing" can be a highly effective tactic. Psychologist Margaret Singer coined this term in her book *Cults in Our Midst* to describe the process of "flattery, verbal seduction, affectionate but usually nonsexual touching, and lots of attention to [the subject's] every remark."[26]

Identity construction as a tool of totalitarian belief can take a variety of pathways. But at the end of the spectrum—the most energized, dangerous form of it—is the so-called mass formation stage: a point of widespread hysteria and delusion where a crowd will do anything demanded by the surging totalitarian beliefs, incapable of questioning their orders.

Mass Formation and Popular Delusion

Over the years I've lived in Manhattan, I've gone through more than my fair share of left-wing protests—sometimes intentionally, sometimes just trying to get around. During the first days of the anti-capitalist Occupy Wall Street protests in 2011, I walked around Zuccotti Park in Manhattan's Financial District—and rooted for the cops the night they cleaned out the encampments with batons and pepper spray. I've moved through mobs of BLM protesters marching down Sixth Avenue holding signs that call cops racists and murderers. After a mass shooting somewhere else in the country, I navigated Midtown's Bryant Park— a sea of protesters holding up anti–gun violence signs. Some of them were holding their small children, who were holding up their *own* signs denouncing assault weapons—despite being incapable of spelling their own names.

They all chant the same slogans, believe the same talking points, and operate like a flash mob. Some will intentionally break the law to get arrested, proving their radical bona fides to those around them. But, in an overwhelming number of cases, these marchers do not know one another, often have very little in common, and are mobilized rapidly. So what brings them together?

Here we return to the French social scientist and philosopher Gustave Le Bon's *The Crowd: A Study of the Popular Mind*, still to this day among the most cited, insightful analyses of crowd psychology. Le Bon introduced the concept that crowds think like religious fanatics who are absolute in their certainty while conducting themselves like a wild beast. Compared with the individuals comprising it, the crowd's moral judgment is impaired. So crowds are capable of violence and crimes that would be unthinkable for any of its individual members.

Carl Jung saw this, too, writing, "Crimes the individual alone could never stand are freely committed by the group."[27] Your average lawyer or software developer wouldn't throw a brick or bottle of urine at a police officer, but as members of a BLM riot they would. And they do.

This form of group hypnosis present in the crowd makes "every sentiment and act . . . contagious to such a degree that an individual readily sacrifices his personal interest to the collective interest," writes Le Bon.[28] A crowd's shared identity is its contagion, "of which it is easy to establish the presence, but that it is not easy to explain. It must be classed among those phenomena of a hypnotic order."[29]

The contagion—the shared identity in a crowd—makes it possible to gather and mobilize. In Le Bon's view, crowds are politically essential to "all the world's masters, all the founders of religions or empires, the apostles of all beliefs, eminent statesmen, and, in a more modest sphere, the mere chiefs of small groups of men," who says Le Bon, "have always been unconscious psychologists."[30]

Writing much more recently than Le Bon, Ghent University professor of clinical psychology Mattias Desmet published *The Psychology of Totalitarianism*, a modern study of mass formation, in 2022. One of the critical insights offered by Desmet is that "the masses believe in the story not because it's accurate but because it creates a new social bond."[31] Essentially, the power of belief as it pertains to mass formation has nothing to do with facts and everything to do with the emotions that it evokes and the sense of belonging that it creates.

Identity construction, at its extreme, results in this kind of mass formation—which is itself a celebration of delusions. The truly totalitarian state of belonging in the group is a place where truth is irrelevant. Total mind control—the kind that would lead the Jonestown cult members to mass suicide or cause the Aum Shinrikyō members to try to exterminate the human race—is possible in this mass formation state.

It's easier to understand why those who want power try to control the identity of others than to imagine why individuals agree to cede their identity. When not faced with torture or becoming a hostage, why would people surrender their individuality so freely—especially in the context of a cult, which, while mentally coercive, usually lacks the force of secret police and prison camps?

We may tell ourselves otherwise, but the truth is human beings like to be told what to do. To much of the world, choice and freedom are frightening concepts. Although totalitarianism discourse revolves around incidents of brute force to coerce belief, not everyone requires a pistol pointed at their face to confess a lie. Some just need to be told that everyone else is confessing the lie, too.

And group identity comes with its privileges. Meerloo writes of this desire to join the crowd:

In exchange for giving up his individuality, he obtains some special gratifications: the feeling of belonging and of being protected, the sense of relief over losing his personal boundaries and responsibilities, the ecstasy of being taken up and absorbed in wild, uncontrolled collective feelings, the safety of being anonymous, of being merely a cog in the wheel of the all-powerful state.[32]

This also describes the appeal of the most insular religious sects. They take away their followers' choice about most matters of day-to-day life, and paradoxically their followers find freedom in the obedience required. For example, members of religious sects find relief by placing decision-making in the hands of their respective clergy. Rules about everything from food to dress code to sexual habits reinforce the group identity.

Group identity can also offer weak people a shortcut to self-esteem, which can easily cross into arrogance. Eric Hoffer goes so far as to claim that "the less justified a man is in claiming excellence for his own self, the more ready he is to claim all excellence for his nation, his religion, his race or his holy cause."[33] If all one has to do in order to improve his self-worth is adopt totalitarian beliefs—political parties, cults, and backward religions will have an endless source of recruits among the easily led and the undistinguished.

Saul Alinsky, the highly effective, morally reprobate "community organizer" from Chicago and guru to both Hillary Clinton and Barack Obama, recognized this phenomenon. In *Rules for Radicals*, Alinsky wrote that a key recruitment tactic was giving would-be radicals an identity that made them feel worthwhile and full of purpose.

First, he started by targeting the atomized and isolated individual:

> It is a desperate search for personal identity—to let other people know that at least you are alive. Let's take a common case in the ghetto. A man is living in a slum tenement. He doesn't know anybody and nobody knows him. He doesn't care for anyone because no one cares for him. On the corner newsstand are newspapers with pictures of people like Mayor Daley and other people from a different world.[34]

Then Alinsky imagines the recruiter as the savior of this "common case in the ghetto," whom the recruiter can bring into community and out of

> a world that he doesn't know, a world that doesn't know that he is even alive. When the organizer approaches him part of what begins to be communicated is that through the organization and its power he will get his birth certificate for life, that he will become known, that things will

change from the drabness of a life where all that changes is the calendar.[35]

Now, one may argue whether leftist community organizers like Alinsky ever care for the future and long-term self-esteem of their indoctrinated subjects beyond their political utility (I'd say clearly not). But Alinsky was certainly aware of the power he and his followers could gain by constructing ready-made identities for the downtrodden and disaffected.

As such, mass formation and mob mentality remain a common goal of the Left. If, like I was, you were flying in or out of New York City between Christmas 2023 and New Year's, chances are you encountered mobs calling for the destruction of Israel "from the river to the sea," blocking the roads to LaGuardia and JFK Airports. They also blocked the Brooklyn, Manhattan, and Williamsburg Bridges as well as the Holland Tunnel. The next time a mob blocks a bridge or highway as you're trying to pick up your kid or catch your flight, perhaps try to feel pity for its members instead of rage: Someone like Alinsky likely recruited them because of their emptiness, and the new identity they've constructed—and this new kingdom they inhabit—may be all they have.

Antiracist Identity Construction

Most people in America aren't having their identity manipulated through active mob participation. Instead, it's good old ideological indoctrination that is reforming the American people's concept of themselves and their history. And for many, that new identity is completely focused on racism—or, should I say, antiracism.

The goal of the antiracists is to replace our current national identity—which they believe is white supremacy—with a new, race-conscious one. The most popular educators union in America describes white supremacy this way: "While often associated with violence perpetrated by the KKK and other white supremacist groups, it also describes a political ideology and systemic oppression that perpetuates and maintains the social, political, historical and/or industrial white domination."[36] This means—according to the union representing the people who teach our children in public schools—that you are identified as a white supremacist if you think the US should stop illegal immigrants at the border, end racial preferences, and incarcerate criminals.

Even ostensibly apolitical behavior can be identified as white supremacist: Being punctual and accurate—and expecting the same of students or colleagues—is deemed a sign of latent racism.

A list of fifteen white supremacist traits identified by Dr. Tema Okun, who at the time was a co-leader of Duke University's

Teaching for Equity Fellows Program, includes perfectionism, a sense of urgency, "worshipping the written word," and "believing in objectivity."[37]

To combat this perceived scourge of white supremacy, after George Floyd's death in 2020 progressives began scurrying to embrace a relatively new identity construct: that of the *antiracist*—the white supremacist's heroic foil. The concept comes from Ibram X. Kendi's *How to Be an Antiracist*, which has sold millions of copies since 2020. It's assigned reading in many corporations, universities, and even the military.[38]

One of Kendi's spin-off books targeted at children, *Antiracist Baby*, offers rhyming (though metrically obtuse) wisdom such as "Antiracist baby is bred, *not* born. Antiracist baby is raised to make society transform."[39] (Nothing virtue-signals more than gifting an expecting couple a picture book featuring a father with a baby strapped to his chest, both with their fists raised in the air at a protest.) Kendi is a speaking-circuit sensation and the director of the Center for Antiracist Research at Boston University (which was created in 2020 and, despite more than $43 million in donations, produced almost no research and fired more than half its employees in 2023).[40]

For those unfamiliar with the antiracist identity construction, it can be difficult to fathom why Americans—who twice voted for a black president—require so much instruction in how not to be racists.

But antiracists don't believe any of that is enough. Merely renouncing or repudiating racial animus—however genuinely—doesn't make one an antiracist. In fact, the opposite is true. "Only the racist lives by the heartbeat of denial. The antiracist lives by the opposite heartbeat, one that rarely and irregularly sounds in America—the heartbeat of confession," writes Kendi.[41] So someone who thinks he's not racist is a racist, and someone who confesses to racism becomes an antiracist. Guilt, confession, assuming a new identity—the process is baked in.

Further, *Antiracist Baby* "understands that people aren't the problem—policies are."[42] In order to claim the antiracist identity, one must actively oppose policies that—regardless of their intent—allegedly put black people at a disadvantage or reflect negatively upon them as a group. Kendi finds racism in policies pitched as law and order, color-blind, or race neutral. Further, taking aim at voter fraud, illegal immigration, or the achievement gap in student performance is antithetical to antiracism.[43]

To truly exhibit antiracism, one must accept a political orthodoxy as totalitarian as Communism, pitting white-skinned people as the "haves" against the "have-nots" (everyone else).

Objection to any of this stereotyping will identify you as "fragile," a concept popularized by diversity consultant Robin DiAngelo. Your only escape route from the mob, if you are saddled with whiteness, is to own your privilege, confess to being a racist so you can be an antiracist, and commit to being an "ally" of the have-nots. You have to join the group, adopt their identity markers, and disassociate yourself from what you were before—including immutable traits, like the color of your skin. It's the same erase-and-replace playbook of every mind-control tactic.

The framework of "intersectionality," developed by critical race theorist Kimberlé Crenshaw, views overlapping social identities—such as whiteness and maleness—as force multipliers in situations of privilege and oppression. If you are white, able-bodied, heterosexual, cisgender, male, Christian, middle- or owning-class, middle-aged, or English-speaking, you are "privileged"—according to a frightening list of inherited traits compiled by Sherita Golden during her time as the chief diversity officer at Johns Hopkins University's medical center.[44] And the more privileged identities you possess, the more societally problematic you are.

Conversely, if you are a black, handicapped, queer female Muslim, the intersection of these traits intensifies your oppression in a white supremacist culture. Intersectionality, in the opinion of the (white gay male Catholic) writer Andrew Sullivan,

is operating, in Orwell's words, as a "smelly little orthodoxy," and it manifests itself, it seems to me, almost as a religion. It posits a classic orthodoxy through which all of human experience is explained—and through which all speech must be filtered. Its version of original sin is the power of some identity groups over others. To overcome this sin, you need first to confess, i.e., "check your privilege," and subsequently live your life and order your thoughts in a way that keeps this sin at bay. The sin goes so deep into your psyche, especially if you are white or male or straight, that a profound conversion is required.[45]

The clergy of today's antiracism movement stand ready to reconstruct your identity and invite you to join their mob.

Identity construction—as with forced phobia, brainwashing, and other mind-control tactics—cannot operate alone. It depends on some ready-at-hand ideology that tells people who they are and what they should do.

Mass delusion isn't an empty force. It always has driving ideas. And those ideas must be cultivated, spread, and repeated until people get the point (or can't hear anything else).

To do that requires an old form of information warfare that we're bombarded with—even here in the West—every day. And that's called propaganda.

8

Propaganda

The border separating North Korea from South Korea bristles with the menace of guards, barbed wire, and machine guns. Taken from the perspective of the International Space Station, a series of pictures in 2014 show a brilliantly lit South Korea—and North Korea as a sea of blackness.[1] To the north, across the 38th parallel between the Koreas, there's almost no electricity, except for a little spot on the map where the capital, Pyongyang, is located. It's a stark visualization of the difference in two political systems: Free South Korea is a dynamic light show, and totalitarian Communist North Korea is a nightmarish abyss. A story of freedom and tyranny told by electrons.

When I went to the US–Mexico border as a reporter in 2019, the contrast between our nation and our neighbor to the south made me think of the Korea photographs. To the north of the border wall, all I saw was pristine white sand, a marine conservation area, and, five miles in the distance, the quiet town of Imperial Beach. Looking south of the border, I saw Tijuana, Mexico, with all the telltale signs of a developing country's urban chaos: the noise of constantly barking dogs and the droning of cheap generators, poorly constructed, rusty houses in various states of disrepair—and trash thrown everywhere. It wasn't as extreme as the Koreas, to be sure, but the differences were vast nonetheless.

One thing I've noticed—from Africa to the Middle East to Latin America—is that a sure sign of a corrupt country with inept leadership is haphazard sanitation. From the fence line, San Diego County looked like a beach postcard, whereas Tijuana exuded disorder. Mexico is not without spectacular natural beauty and good people, but it is also a country with ultraviolent cities run by organized crime thanks to the cartels. Our border with Mexico is by far more important to the future of America than any other border in the world. It doesn't need to be as militarized as Korea's, but it should be under control.

That's not what I saw years ago. As I toured our border, I found it was lightly patrolled and generally porous. Not as lightly as Canada's, not as heavily as Korea's. It was more like the semi-porous borders I saw in Iraq. Despite all the political wrangling during the Trump administration over "building a wall," the westernmost end of the border wall was really just a dilapidated fence that anyone could easily climb over. It trailed off toward the beach, with the waves gently lapping against its terminus.

"Looks pretty easy to swim around that," I said to my Border Patrol escort.

"Oh, trust me; they've tried plenty of times," he responded, referring to illegal immigrant crossings, "but it's easier to just find a weak spot in the fence."

While Trump was still president the first time around, I spoke with Border Patrol officers about what an expanded wall (which would, in actuality, be a steel fence) could help them accomplish. They told me it would allow the more efficient deployment of resources, raising the cost of illegal trafficking for the cartels and changing the calculation for those illegal aliens looking to make a run for it. It would slow the transit of drugs and humans in high-traffic areas—often long enough for Border Patrol to make arrests and make Americans safer.

Though it's difficult to tabulate the number of illegal aliens incarcerated at the state level, at the federal level about 15 percent of all those in Bureau of Prisons custody are non-citizens.[2] In 2020, 94 percent of those non-citizens were illegal aliens, according to the Department of Justice, and only 31 percent were in prison for breaking immigration laws. The rest were there for drugs, weapons, racketeering, fraud, or other crimes. A combined 5.6 percent of them included the kidnappers, terrorists, "murderers," and "rapists" that President Donald Trump was attacked for calling out as really *bad hombres*.[3]

The officers patrolling the border said a wall would clearly help. Common sense says a wall would help. But domestic politics demanded that Democrats maintain the abjectly moronic position that a border wall was useless, and they've trumpeted that propaganda enthusiastically for years. Then Speaker of the House Nancy Pelosi said that walls were "immoral."[4] "Here's Why Trump's Border Wall Won't Work,"[5] an op-ed in the Associated Press insisted. *Foreign Policy* magazine picked up the party line with a "Walls Don't Work" piece.[6]

Of course a wall isn't foolproof, but neither is a locked door. Or a safe. Or security cameras. Yet people all over the world still lock their doors and safes and put up security cameras to prevent theft. To undermine the Trump proposition that a wall would be a useful tool to secure the border, the Left selectively applied a new standard to the word *works*: 100 percent efficacy, 100 percent of the time. Their anti-wall rhetoric has influenced national policy for years, but it's all propaganda. And so are all their major positions on the issues of border security and illegal immigration.

The Immigration War over Words

After 2019, I continued to make border trips to El Paso and McAllen, Texas, to report on the lawlessness of human smuggling and the growing power of Mexico's vicious transnational drug cartels. In El Paso, I saw hundreds of people who had surrendered themselves to law enforcement as soon as they illegally entered onto US soil. Of the ones who surrender, around 80 percent will qualify for an asylum application, and nearly 20 percent will be approved.[7] The process can take almost six years—a time in which they can remain in the United States—which is why many make no effort to evade Border Patrol. They get six years living where they want anyway while they wait to accomplish their ultimate goal of permanent residency. So they flag down our officers, repeat the phrases that their cartel smugglers train them to say in order to get in process for asylum, and get released into the US interior to wait.

Border Patrol members told me that this process had become standard; officers went from, well, patrolling the border to merely serving as a "welcoming committee" for illegal aliens. Whatever law enforcement function they were supposed to provide was completely overshadowed by the "humanitarian mission" of making sure everyone who crossed illegally was safe and fed and had a bed to sleep in. This was intentionally exploited on a systematic scale. In the "sanctuary city" of New York, it is now common to read reports of illegal aliens punching cops,[8] panhandling,[9] and shooting Times Square tourists while shoplifting.[10]

This slow-rising crisis has reached such a breaking point that a majority of Americans now support Trump's policies of mass deportations. But this is *in spite* of what Democrats and the old-guard corporate news media are telling them. When it comes to illegal immigration, we have been lied to constantly for decades. The title of John F. Kennedy's 1958 book, *A Nation of Immigrants*, has been repeated ad nauseam by politicians who favor open borders—whether it's because they want less expensive labor or more Democratic voters. "A nation of immigrants" has become propaganda aimed at softening our view of illegal aliens, no matter their qualifications or intent. We are supposed to think that settlers who arrived here in an untamed wilderness and built their homes and towns with their own hands are somehow analogous to third-world arrivals today who get welfare right away. If we must now accept all immigrants from any country in whatever amount, what's the point of having any immigration laws?

Those who borrow Kennedy's talking points don't bother to acknowledge that for most of the twentieth century, we were not a nation of immigrants. According to Pew Research, as summarized by the National Institute of Corrections, "Since 1965, when U.S. immigration laws replaced a national quota system, the number of immigrants living in the U.S. has more than quadrupled. Immigrants today account for 13.7 percent of the U.S. population, nearly triple the share (4.8 percent) in 1970."[11]

While we might have a rough idea of how many legal immigrants live in the US, we have no idea how many illegal aliens are here. The Office of Immigration Statistics estimated in 2020 that there were around eleven million illegal immigrants in the United States.[12] The government prints this information to be taken seriously, despite the fact that the same Census Bureau data estimated there were 10.8 million illegal immigrants in the United States in 2010.[13] We're to believe that between 2010 and 2020 the US netted only two hundred thousand illegal immigrants? That fiction, of course, has been blown away by the estimated ten million illegal crossings that occurred during the Biden administration.

Whenever I asked Border Patrol agents about this estimate, they would laugh. They were encountering hundreds of thousands of illegal alien entries a month, and somehow the total number barely budged?[14] How could anyone in the government or media believe the preposterous official estimate of only eleven million illegals living in America after decades of lawlessness at the border? For that number to be accurate we'd have to see massive caravans of illegal aliens leaving America every month, not the other way around.

Pew Research estimates, "As of 2021, the nation's 10.5 million unauthorized immigrants represented about 3 percent of the total U.S. population and 22 percent of the foreign-born population."[15] Considering illegal immigrants make up 15 percent of our federal prison population, red flags should be flying up. According to their own numbers, migrants are disproportionately imprisoned for committing crimes.

But if you google "immigrants and crime," you're treated to a list of gleeful treatises that claim to prove immigrants commit fewer crimes than the native born. This is why so many Democrats demand the erasure of the word *illegal* for opaque words like *undocumented*—a change of language blurs the distinctions between those who enter legally and those who don't while ignoring the fraudulent abuses of our asylum system (not to mention the fact that when aliens cross our border without our approval, they are committing a crime . . . which is "illegal").

All of this manipulation of data and language is a clear propaganda campaign deployed by advocates of illegal immigration against the American people. And for decades it worked! Before President Trump's second term, when the border was finally secured, tens of thousands of illegal aliens crossed the border each month, but the Left refuses to let us even call it what it is. But thankfully, a solid majority of Americans have woken up to the realities of this invasion.

Of course, the Left doesn't just bombard the American people with propaganda on illegal immigration. Every time we're told Trump is a fascist, men can have periods, crime is the fault of the victim, J6ers are insurrectionists, BLM rioters are heroes, there's nothing weird about a grown man dressed in a thong sexually dancing in front of a child, and every other insane statement that comes from modern progressives, we're being fed propaganda.

Propaganda styles vary, depending on the power and intent of the machinery generating it. But while the more extreme pathways of mind control—conditioning, menticide, reeducation—generally require a level of state-backed force that is absent in a free society—everyone everywhere is subject to propaganda. If totalitarian menticide is a bubonic plague of the mind, then propaganda is a highly infectious cold virus.

It doesn't matter if you've had your mind wiped clean or not. For some reason, some people are able to fight propaganda off without much trouble (chances are if you're reading this book, you're one of them). But billions of others are immediately susceptible. And that's dangerous, because propaganda can suddenly morph into something much more dangerous, causing mass hysteria and mass delusions.

That's the power of propaganda run amok: It is an endless stream of lies, it's everywhere, it's inescapable, and it can make entire societies go crazy.

Propaganda as a Psychological Operation

As a radio show host, I have a particular love for the medium. There's something intimate about radio. At its purest, it's a one-to-one conversation between the speaker and millions of listeners at the same time. But as a trained intelligence officer, I'm well aware that in history radio has played a dark role as a powerful tool of propaganda. Like social media, print journalism, TV, and every medium, radio can be used for good or evil. It depends on who is propagating what on it.

Controlling the minds of the masses with outright lies spread across an entire country at once became technologically feasible shortly after the ingenious Italian Guglielmo Marconi invented the wireless radio in the 1890s. Radios could spread needed news, sports broadcasts, and enjoyable shows. But it was also the single biggest change in technology that aided the spread of totalitarian propaganda at the turn of the century, beginning slowly in World War I and reaching perception-dominance levels over the course of World War II.

"It fell to the Germans to develop the manipulation of public opinion into a huge, well-organized machine. Their psychological warfare became aggressive strategy in peacetime, the so-called war between wars," Joost Meerloo wrote.[16]

In 1933, Joseph Goebbels, Hitler's propaganda minister, plainly admitted, "We make no bones about the fact that the radio belongs to us and to no one else. . . . I consider radio to be the most modern and the most crucial instrument that exists for influencing the masses."[17] The Third Reich encouraged the development of lower-cost radio receivers so every household could afford one.

Deutsche Welle correspondent Christoph Hasselbach wrote of the effects: "It isn't far-fetched to say that radio helped start the war. On September 1, 1939, Germans heard a report about a Polish attack. That was fake, of course, but it allowed Hitler to take to the airwaves to announce that fighting was underway. Germany invaded Poland under false pretenses."[18]

Here in the United States, American radio ownership was also skyrocketing during the 1930s, reaching around 90 percent of the total population by 1940.[19] Despite initial reluctance to build a government propaganda machine, the US established the Office of War Information in 1942—after Pearl Harbor was attacked and America could no longer sit out the war. It seems odd to us now that Americans would be so open to obvious government information manipulation. But the truth is propaganda had been around for millennia—and it didn't always have a negative association.

Without question, the use of deception to confuse enemies and control populations is as old as civilization itself. The Chinese military philosopher Sun Tzu wrote over two thousand years ago in *The Art of War*, "All warfare is based on deception."[20]

Throughout human history, savvy warriors have used disinformation, spy networks, and rumors to gain a battlefield advantage. Military leaders from Caesar to Napoleon used such deception to create vast empires.

However, the intentional use of lying not just in military affairs but to control populations on a mass scale is a more modern phenomenon. Before Johannes Gutenberg's invention of the printing press in the mid-fifteenth century, there was no efficient way to spread propaganda through writing, and for centuries afterward the limitations on public literacy and the dissemination of physical texts created additional difficulties.

It was after Gutenberg and the descent of Europe into schism that the word *propaganda* itself was brought into more popular usage in the Catholic Church, through its response to the spread of Protestantism. Mark Crispin Miller writes in his introduction to Edward Bernays's book *Propaganda* that in 1622 "Pope Gregory XV . . . urgently proposed an addition to the Roman curia. The Office for the Propagation of the Faith (*Congregatio de propaganda fide*) would supervise the Church's missionary efforts."[21] So the original propaganda was supposed to aid the spread of absolute truth.

Yet today when we hear "propaganda," we think of foreign dictatorships and ham-fisted state media slavishly praising the regime. We don't necessarily think of religious tracts or even slanted news stories or selective reporting. But really it's all propaganda. Whether we're talking about a totalitarian society or a constitutional republic, propaganda is present. It's just a question of degree.

The pro-Putin lies printed in *Pravda* (ironically, Russian for "truth") may be more overt than the sympathetic coverage of Democrats in *The New York Times* today, but the basic propaganda tactics are the same. Left-wing interest groups pitch stories to left-wing reporters and editors who produce fantastical stories about the looming climate catastrophe brought on by the US's fossil fuel industry, the systemic racism responsible for police shooting unarmed black men, or the epidemic of children killing themselves because their backward parents aren't supportive enough of their gender fluidity. Counterpoints are excluded, marginalized, or mocked. If you aren't aware, you don't even know you're being fed a narrative, not the news.

We can see the results. Today, more than two-thirds of Americans are "somewhat or extremely anxious" about climate,[22] a clear majority believe racism is a major issue,[23] and pediatric referrals to transgender clinics increased 504 percent between 2015 and 2018.[24] In America, we aren't manipulated by browbeating praises of the cultural regime. We're lulled into thinking there simply is no alternative to the "kind," "correct," and "respectable" opinions of the ruling class.

Is it possible for the masses to hear so much propaganda, day in and day out, that they will believe anything? The history of modern propaganda tells us, unfortunately, yes. The introduction of radio and eventually television led Meerloo to believe that propaganda had advanced so much that:

> Mass delusion can be induced. It is simply a question of organizing and manipulating collective feelings in the proper way. If one can isolate the mass, allow no free thinking, no free exchange, no outside corrective, and hypnotize the group daily with noises, with press and radio and television, with fear and pseudo-enthusiasms, any delusion can be instilled.[25]

Once it became possible to reach mass audiences, propagandists had the reach to lie to people endlessly and weaponize words themselves. And those are two of the tactics that most define the modern tactics of propaganda: lie repetition and language manipulation.

Lie Repetition: "Firehose of Falsehood"

When Russia invaded Ukraine in February 2022—and encountered fierce resistance they weren't expecting—many observers predicted Vladimir Putin would be ousted as president for starting an unpopular war. There were rumblings of a coup in the highest ranks of the military and inside the Kremlin.

How could Putin survive the wrath of the masses, whose husbands and sons were disappearing into his meat grinder?

The answer? Absolutely relentless, nonstop propaganda.

Night and day, Russian state media and its social media organs tirelessly spread the lie that its troops were fighting Nazism in Ukraine. When Russian propaganda shifted and began characterizing the invasion as a counterterrorist operation, the intensity and frequency of the propaganda didn't let up. Media coverage of Russian clergy blessing troops painted the invasion as a battle of good versus evil. Russians who couldn't speak multiple languages or simply move abroad to avoid the draft bought it. The Ukrainians, for their part, also mobilized wartime propaganda over the ensuing years of conflict.

There's no more transformative power over public opinion than the ability to make the masses believe lies. "Pavlovian conditioning to special words forces people into an automatic thinking that is tied to those words. The words we use influence our behavior in daily life; they determine the thoughts we have,"[26] Meerloo explained. Pushing lies is at the heart of conditioning, weaponized law, forced phobia, isolation, and brainwashing. And it is the centerpiece of propaganda.

This is why totalitarians devote so much effort to state media, militarized pageantry, and the mythology of the regime. The totalitarian propagandist sees all communication as an opportunity to further the state's hold on the public mind. No one

knows this better than Putin, a trained KGB officer who operated in East Germany during the Cold War. Meerloo observed,
"The totalitarians organize intensive dialectical training for
their subjects lest their doubts get the better of them. They try
to do the same thing to the rest of the world in a less obtrusive
way."[27]

In 2008, during Putin's four-year hiatus away from the presidency (he still retained power, he simply moved to a different
position to respect a semblance of constitutional legitimacy),
Russian president Dmitry Medvedev led an invasion of Georgia
and took 20 percent of its territory—claiming he was protecting Russian citizens from the atrocities of Georgian aggressors.
Georgia, however, hired a public relations firm and launched a
successful counterinformation campaign—blocking Russian propaganda and reporting on civilians targeted by Russians. "Ultimately, Georgia gained the upper hand in the information
conflict, a fact corroborated by Russia's review of its military's
performance, which noted deficiencies in both the information-
technical and information-psychological domains," writes cy-
berintelligence analyst Emilio J. Iasiello.[28]

Putin resumed the presidency in 2012 and invaded Crimea
in 2014. Under his leadership, and in the era of social media
and smartphones, Russian war propaganda would be much
more sophisticated. "The Russian 'Firehose of Falsehood' Propaganda Model," a Rand Corporation research paper by Chris-

topher Paul and Miriam Matthews, looks back at the evolution of information operations in Russia since its 2008 invasion of Georgia and observes that in some ways, "the current Russian approach to propaganda builds on Soviet Cold War–era techniques, with an emphasis on obfuscation and on getting targets to act in the interests of the propagandist without realizing that they have done so. In other ways, it is completely new and driven by the characteristics of the contemporary information environment."[29]

So Putin's Russia has taken old-school, KGB-style information warfare and updated it for the internet. This evolution of Russian propaganda, according to the Rand study, has four primary characteristics:

1. High-volume and multichannel
2. Rapid, continuous, and repetitive
3. Lacks commitment to objective reality
4. Lacks commitment to consistency[30]

Endlessly blasting lies from every available avenue, no matter how egregiously dishonest or contradictory: That's the formula for Russia's "firehose of falsehood." In a world of smartphones and constant connectivity, the ability for today's leaders to saturate the public has no comparison in all of human history. And it's not just President Putin who is putting on a propaganda master class. Malevolent actors around the world—in Venezuela, North Korea, Iran, etc.—are borrowing from the Putin playbook and successfully fomenting mass delusions. According to a report by Joan Donovan at *Time* magazine, in 2020 the Oxford Internet Institute found eighty-one countries "with active cyber troop operations [that were] utilizing many different strategies to spread false information, including spending millions on online advertising."

While the rapidly evolving technologies of encrypted chat apps, social media platforms, and artificial technology are dazzling and new, the efficacy of the "firehose of falsehood" is rooted in fundamental human psychology. Meerloo observed how constant, brutally forceful messaging could weaken resistance in the listener: "Expressed in psychoanalytic terms, through daily propagandistic noise backed up by forceful verbal cues, people can more and more be forced to identify with the powerful noisemaker. Big Brother's voice resounds in all the little brothers."[31]

Overwhelming the subject with false messages is critical. Meerloo describes propaganda used in the process of menticide as "indoctrination barrage," a constant pressuring of the subject with ideological orthodoxy.[32] The volume of the indoctrination is meant to be a flood, unstoppable as it bounces around the brain's synapses.

The "firehose of falsehood" used in the public arena is

meant to manipulate similar neurological pathways as "indoctrination barrage" imposed on subjects of menticide.

But the firehose of falsehood is about more than unrelenting repetition. This type of propaganda also deals in lies. This creates intentional confusion in the target and over time undermines their intellectual dignity. Meerloo learned from his time countering the Nazi Third Reich that:

> Every human communication can be either a report of straight facts or an attempt to suggest things and situations as they do not exist. Such distortion and perversion of facts strike at the core of human communication. The verbal battle against man's concept of truth and against his mind seems to be ceaseless.[33]

This struggle between lie and truth can be subtly pernicious: the silly uniforms of Castro or Mao, the goose-stepping military parades, and the massive posters of the dear leader deepen the manufactured public image of the regime. But that kind of garish display is necessary to the assault on truth. People living in sophisticated Western democracies are subject to the same "firehose of falsehood" even without totalitarian parades.

Supposedly honest institutions can peddle lies in ways that are imperceptible to most of the public but still shape their perceptions and push them to embrace lies. Take the example of "objective journalism" in the US. For decades, Americans were force-fed an absurd line that journalism was 'nonpartisan.' It's now well established that most corporate journalism is effectively an outgrowth of the Democrat Party. A Syracuse University study in 2022 found that only 3 percent of journalists nationwide identify as Republicans—versus 36 percent who self-identify as Democrat.[34] In reality, almost every journalist who does not openly identify as a Republican is effectively a Democrat (or a Communist).

Media bias isn't new. Since the country's founding, American newspapers with contrasting political opinions feuded with each other, and pamphleteers were at one another's throats because of conflicting ideas. But it was the rise of mass media technology in the twentieth century and the consolidation of media power in the hands of corporations like ABC, CBS, and NBC (as well as the declining number of newspapers and, eventually, a few cable outlets) that allowed a one-size-fits-all model to promulgate. The public once knew the diverse newspapers of old were filled with opinions. When the "news" was consolidated, we were told what we got was "objective."

Protected by their status as "objective journalists," social justice warriors parading as chroniclers of the facts shaped and set the narrative of public policy issues—resulting in one of the Left's most successful psychological operations in the last hundred years. Night after night, left-wing "firehose"-style propaganda was aimed into the living rooms of Americans across the country, who were none the wiser.

This media stranglehold continued, until eventually, and very recently, the fever broke. "Massive public manipulation," Elon Musk responded on Twitter (now X) on May 9, 2023.[35] The owner of the social media platform X, founder of SpaceX, and cofounder-CEO of Tesla was responding to a chart created by an account called The Rabbit Hole showing that the usage of the words *racist*, *racists*, and *racism* had exploded at four of the largest newspapers in America right around 2014,[36] the year that Michael Brown was shot and killed by police in Ferguson, Missouri.

Musk's conclusion was broadly shared by many of his then more than 170 million followers on X. Why, suddenly, did the legacy media begin fixating on racism in 2014 and not let up? What changed? Did America suddenly become much more racist? That proposition is completely counterintuitive. The reality is that the establishment media chose a propaganda line, and they were going to relentlessly push it on the population. The Rabbit Hole account commented on this graphic: "If Legacy Media is going to shove bigotry porn down our throats it should at least do so in an honest manner so people can have an accurate understanding of racial dynamics."[37]

The word *racist* was weaponized propaganda: It was a way

to dismiss President Donald Trump and his supporters without having to engage with them. As Hillary Clinton said of her opponent's supporters, they're "racist, sexist, homophobic, xenophobic, Islamophobic—you name it."[38]

The propaganda worked, at least for a while, among the easily programmed. After Americans were subjected to a firehose of stories about racism, it impacted their beliefs about immigration, crime, education, and economics, all of which are scrutinized relentlessly for evidence of racism. Pew Research polling in 2017 suggested that the share of Americans who viewed racism as a "big problem" almost doubled from 2011 to 2017, rising from 28 percent to 58 percent.[39]

America didn't suddenly become a more racist place over those years. What changed was the narrative. America and its institutions are systemically racist, they told us, because that served the media and Democrat party's political purposes.

Obviously, one of the most effective ways the media—in a free or totalitarian state—can achieve such a hypnotizing effect is through an endless stream of lies. But there's an even more insidious form of deception than telling lies: making words themselves part of the lie.

Language Manipulation: Loaded Words

Don't call it a war. Call it a liberation or special operation, the Kremlin assuredly told Russian media as the Ukraine invasion unfolded. Dictating which words may be used is another way the totalitarian propagandist undermines facts. Words are the building blocks for our communication, and often our thoughts. Thousands have been prosecuted for "discrediting" the Russian army, for saying the wrong thing under censorship laws adopted a week after Russia "liberated" Ukraine.

The narratives that unfold in our minds are the result of how words are assembled—which words are chosen and which are excluded. As the pieces of the puzzle change, the narrative changes.

This can happen coercively, as with Ivan Pavlov when he induced physical responses in dogs triggered by auditory controls. A tyrant can break a person down with truncheons and electric shocks, convincing the hapless victim through pain response to mouth the mandatory slogans of the state. Conditioning through extreme physical stimuli—beatings, imprisonment, isolation—certainly accelerate the process of mind control. But when using soft power—propaganda—the manipulation of words can be similarly effective in controlling people's minds, at least over time. And it can all be done without the police-state messiness of gulags and mass murder.

After all, how many people today mouth the lies of the corporate media without ever having been explicitly threatened to do so, or else?

Dr. Meerloo remarked of propaganda that it offered a means whereby the "terrorizing force can finally be replaced by a new organization of the means of communication."[40]

Meerloo saw words replicating the effect of the buzzer Dr. Pavlov used to condition his canine subjects, albeit in a more subtle way. "Pavlov had already explained," Meerloo writes, "that man's relation to the external world, and to his fellow men, is dominated by secondary stimuli, the speech symbols. Man learns to think in words and in the speech figures given him, and these gradually condition his entire outlook on life and on the world."[41]

To a degree, Meerloo was oversimplifying the ability to condition people with words. Humans are not dogs; our minds are far more complicated. Even well-conditioned dogs kept in environmentally controlled cages presented Dr. Pavlov with an experience that was frequently humbling and befuddling. The dogs' varying degrees of obedience and anxiety reflected their unique personalities, and yielded differences in experimental outcomes.

So the masses aren't quite Pavlov's dogs . . . but our brains do have weaknesses that propagandists constantly exploit. And we can't ignore the subconscious training our brain receives when bombarded with specific narratives or when particular words are twisted into lies. Meerloo's summary of the situation was: "he who dictates and formulates the words and phrases we use, he who is master of the press and radio, is master of the mind."[42]

The twentieth century marked the implementation of the tools of mass delusion on a population-wide scale. Now in the twenty-first century these tools can be perfected with technologies that the tyrants of the last century would never have dreamed of.

Psychological manipulation, torture, firehoses of falsehoods, gulags—these are all blunt means directed to the elusive end of controlling others' minds.

But emerging technologies—some already on the market today—are much more insidious and influential. They have the power to more effectively change not only what we think— but perhaps even how we think.

The Future of Mass Delusion

It was the first time I'd ever seen a black George Washington.

I'd typed "founding fathers" into the search engine, and an image of George Washington came back—white, powdered wig, Colonial attire—except he was no longer Caucasian. The first president of the United States was suddenly black.

It was February 2024, and I was experimenting with Google's new Gemini Artificial Intelligence (AI) image generator. It was hard to believe that the stories about the new "woke AI" were true because it was so brazen. But sure enough, they were. Something, or someone, over at Google had made it possible that when anyone wants to see an image of the Founding Fathers, they would be shown as black men. And that wasn't all.

I tried to search for various historical figures, some of the most famous popes (until Pope Francis, essentially all of whom were European), and pretty much all famous historical figures were coming up on search results as black.

It caused quite an uproar. Gemini was off to a rough start. How could this have happened to one of the most technologically advanced companies in the world?

It was all an accident, they said. The expected corporate apologies flowed. Alphabet (the parent company of Google) assured consumers that this wasn't some DEI algorithm run amok. It was merely some early bugs in the code still being worked out.[1] Nothing to see here, folks.

I didn't believe the excuses. There's certainly no reason to give the Silicon Valley titans any benefit of the doubt. Google—especially through its subsidiary YouTube, an online video platform that takes up 11 percent of global traffic[2]—has firmly established left-wing political biases. In what they elevate and suppress, Google and YouTube are two of the most powerful propaganda (and mind-control) tools on the planet.

I remember during Covid having my commentaries about masks (which don't work) and vaccine mandates (also don't work) censored or limited by the partisan hacks running the YouTube "trust and safety" department. That was on top of all the reports of skewed search results, blacklisting, and more. It convinced me there may be no more insidious threat to free speech in the twenty-first century than the censorship commissars working for major social media platforms.

But the concern over "Black George Washington" stretches far beyond a single early version of an image-creation tool. With the emergence of AI, our perception of reality is increasingly at risk. Those who control AI—or perhaps even AI itself—will be using an immeasurably powerful tool to condition, brainwash, enforce phobias, and construct new identities upon us. What we think of as real will soon come under assault in ways previous generations couldn't have imagined.

Just think about the possibilities: Bad actors manipulate votes by convincingly creating compromising materials of a political candidate with AI. False videos of a senator spewing racial epithets, for example, could go viral days before voting begins. Or the CEO of a company could be shown on video groping a female subordinate, leading to his removal. The video itself could seem genuine—difficult or even impossible for human eyes or ears to detect as a fake. Elections could be swayed. Public reputations ruined, especially to target those disfavored by the regime. We're only just beginning to grasp the power of these deepfakes, as they're generally called.

While this technology is still evolving, its widespread availability is inevitable. And it will undoubtedly be used as a weapon of information warfare.

We've seen early indicators of how those in power purposefully foment distrust of what we see, read, or hear. Going back to 2016, the Democrats used "fake news" as an epithet to attack pro-Trump posts online, especially on Facebook. The Democrat-aligned legacy media claimed that the stories Trump supporters liked were Russian fakes. The prevalence of such fakes was greatly exaggerated—they were incredibly clumsy and easy to spot. The entire exercise was meant to give left-wing elites an opportunity to sneer at Republicans and sow distrust.

Then Trump flipped the "fake news" accusation around, using it to describe correctly the unrepentant, dishonest partisan corporate media. The media responded by deploying the term *disinformation* against Trump and his supporters, which we've learned means any opinion or fact that hurts Democrats politically.

Ironically, those who scream "disinformation" the loudest are like every would-be mind controller out there. They employ lies while accusing others of wrongdoing.

The ill-fated Biden reelection campaign, for example, tried to leverage AI fears for its own benefit back in 2024. As videos showing Biden in clear cognitive decline rocketed around the internet, White House Press Secretary Karine Jean-Pierre deployed the term *cheap fakes*. Instead of acknowledging the truth of Biden's obvious senility, the apparatus around him tried to denounce the truth as tech-enabled lies. Eventually, Biden would be shoved out of the 2024 presidential race when his cognitive decline became too obvious to hide. The term *cheap fakes* was abandoned, just like Biden's campaign of dementia deception.

The Union of Technology and Mind Control

AI could be the most insidious manipulation technology that's been created. But advances in mind control and technology—especially in mass media—have gone in parallel for hundreds of years. Without mass media, mass delusion is almost impossible to achieve. Sophisticated indoctrination efforts imposed on large nation-states could begin only after the introduction of Gutenberg's printing press in the fifteenth century. New advances—from radio to TV to the internet—allowed indoctrination to reach totalitarian levels.

Without posters and printing presses elevating collective farms, factories, and the glories of revolution, Stalin's rapacious security services might have been unable to command public obedience in the early years of the Soviet Union. Mao Tse-tung formally announced the formation of the People's Republic of China to two hundred thousand listeners in Tiananmen Square—and simultaneously broadcast the speech on radio. Mao would rely heavily on radio as a brainwashing tool for the peasants of China, building more than ten thousand radio receiving stations across the mainland and erecting loudspeakers at these locations to bombard everyone in every possible village or town with Marxist dogma.[3]

Television was the next major innovation added to the mass delusion toolbox. Every totalitarian society strictly controls what broadcasts are allowed on TV, especially anything with cultural influence. Communist TV behind the Iron Curtain during the Cold War was clumsy, but as the only programming available, it had considerable impact on mass perception.

The internet allowed for a fine-tuning of mind-control tactics, far exceeding what the printing press, radio, and TV made possible before. Of course, there are many incredible impacts of the worldwide web—but there are dark sides to it as well. China uses the internet as a tool of mass control, with its "great firewall" blocking a significant number of outside sites and an Orwellian social credit system rating its population through every interconnected action and transaction.

North Korea is still so poor and backward that the internet is reserved only for the elites. It has an intranet called the Kwangmyong, which is heavily monitored, has only a few thousand sites, and is essentially a propaganda repository. But the North Korean national security apparatus still maintains a sophisticated nation-state hacking capability that it will deploy to intimidate critics around the world.

Here at home, the internet remains a frontline battlefield for freedom. Most Americans have woken up to the reality that our usage of the web comes at the steep price of our privacy. Technology giants track every site we visit, our physical locations, and our tastes in everything from movies to pretzels. This trove of our digital information retained by private companies vastly surpasses whatever microfilms the East German Stasi compiled on dissidents in Communist Germany. Right now, information gathered from our internet usage is used for hyper-targeted advertising. Of course, it could easily be manipulated to influence our psychological weak points, twist our perceptions of reality, isolate us from our friends and family, and impose upon us a revised conception of reality. Knowledge is power, and we freely give this knowledge about ourselves away.

Truth be told, the internet is the most impressive surveillance and propaganda dissemination device in the history of our species—by far. Yet, despite having had such technology for years, we are only just beginning to understand the implications of billions of people carrying in their pockets more power than the supercomputers of forty years ago.

With artificial intelligence, we're on the precipice of a technological revolution that could transform humanity beyond what the internet is capable of. Even outside of deepfakes, the implications are enormous. AI could become far more granular and accurate in polling, for example, than anything humans have been able to do with phone calls and push polls. Will AI be able to write legislation, then get a vote in Congress and head to the president's desk for signature? What about an AI program that comes up with a political platform, finds ways to make money, and builds its own party?

AI could become a tool of super-propaganda, micro-targeting individuals millions of times over to sway public opinion. Instead of door-knocking humans and volunteers sealing envelopes at campaign headquarters, it could be an algorithm making realistic-sounding robocalls plus supercharging narratives online with search function and display ads. The applications are endless.

It's not hard to see how this technological power could be weaponized as a tool to implement totalitarian delusion—just as legacy media have been so used in the past. If a handful of social media companies can (and, I would argue, have) shifted presidential election results over the last decade, there's every reason to believe a dominant AI company could manipulate public perception at scale to sway our democracy.

This makes something seemingly silly or innocuous like a "woke" AI image generator so troubling. When the Soviets wanted to rewrite history, they would go about retouching executed party members out of photographs. They used razor blades to cut names out of state documents. It was clumsy, time-consuming, and impossible to replicate at scale. No matter how hard Stalin tried—it was impossible to erase names from every government document, newspaper, and photocopy.

But AI changes that. A powerful enough AI program could remove stories and photos from existence on the web or even replace them with new images that adhere to the desired political orthodoxy. For the general public, it will be impossible to know that anything is amiss. They will see what they always see on their screens and assume the system is working as it always has.

A bit further into our tech future—but visible on the horizon—lie brain-computer Interfaces (BCIs), such as Elon Musk's Neuralink. Neuralink is already accomplishing what seemed like the stuff of science fiction only a few decades ago with "fully implantable, cosmetically invisible [devices] . . . designed to let you control a computer or mobile device anywhere you go," as the company describes it.[4] Neuralink BCI devices have successfully allowed a human being to move a computer mouse with thoughts.[5] It's just the beginning.

Without question, there are wondrous medical uses for BCIs. It now seems only a matter of time before people who have been paralyzed, for example, will be able to use a BCI to control their wheelchairs, computers, and robotic prosthetics with their thoughts. Neuralink also has a program called Blindsight—which has received a "breakthrough device" designation from the Food and Drug Administration[6]—that hopes to restore vision to people who are blind, including those who have lost both eyes. If the patient has an undamaged visual cortex, Neuralink is hoping to let the blind see.

As with any great technological advance, BCIs bring up complicated ethical questions. Our minds are the last refuge of autonomy in a world of smartphones and constant surveillance. As we've seen time and again, technology that we can manipulate can be used to manipulate us. The mere fact that BCIs will transform how we receive and process information means they'll become another major battlefield of mind control by state and nonstate actors alike.

That's the other side of the coin. BCIs in the wrong hands could become truly dystopian. If an implant in the brain is powerful enough to control elements of the physical world, will it also enable memories to be wiped or implanted? Will it be possible to control human behavior not through a collection of repeated stimuli or even external coercion but through direct electronic signals to the brain? *The Manchurian Candidate* trope could rapidly go from an exaggerated sci-fi thriller to a medical reality.

For all his scientific genius, Pavlov's theories and observations on classical conditioning work on a primitive level. Conditioning amounts to a baseline scientific understanding that our minds affect our bodies, and vice versa, in quantifiable ways. Building upon Pavlov's research, the cynical pioneers of every other tool of mind control psychologically battled against the reality that subjects had known was the case—through their upbringing, their history, their education, and everything else around them. Totalitarians used often brutal tactics to attempt to traumatize people and erase their former selves, all so they could impose new identities and ideologies in place of the old.

But soon enough totalitarian regimes may not even need to condition our responses, kill our minds, weaponize the law against us, or use any other terrorizing means of mass delusion. Like today's North Koreans, the next generation could be born into a world where those in power will manipulate reality to their liking—only instead of using gulags and propaganda, they use AI and BCIs. Raised in a lie, human beings could be brainwashed en masse without even knowing it.

Today we're more reliant on the ability to "google" something than ever before. For many people, if something doesn't exist online, it's hard to believe it exists at all. Enabled by AI and BCIs, the methods of mind control may soon be able to move beyond conditioning, brainwashing, indoctrination, and propaganda to a more mechanistic level of mastery. If AI shapes perception and can even falsify evidence online in a convincing way, who's to say what the truth really is? If our brain can be technologically induced to love or hate, feel fear or euphoria, to stop or to obey at the metaphorical flip of a switch, it's game over.

That said, the technology isn't there yet. Some of the prognostications about breakthroughs could be overblown. A world of BCIs that control the mind instead of the mechanics of an arm or leg could be much further off. Even when it comes to AI, experts continue to debate whether machine learning will only create conveniences and efficiencies in the short term while leaving true societal transformation decades or more out.

However long it takes, the promethean nature of these scientific discoveries is inescapable. Nuclear fission begets nuclear weapons. Radio begets mass media. There's no denying at least the possibility that the last refuge of autonomy—our minds—will become increasingly subject to the encroachment of technology. "Brainwashing" would no longer be a colorful description of a complicated process. It could be neurological reality.

All of this poses challenges for the future of humanity. As machine learning and BCIs become more sophisticated, it is even more incumbent on individuals and society at large to stay rooted in truth and fact. As individuals, we can't control technological advancement. So the best way to prepare for this coming cyber-reality is to understand the tactics used to control our minds today and think, as we have in these pages, how to respond to the ways technology can deepen mental intrusions. The battle to maintain our psychological autonomy has only just begun.

It Can Happen Here

We are always closer to a mass delusion than the masses realize.

The mob is powerful but never self-aware. As we've seen from Communism to Covid, groups of people can be pushed toward self-destruction in the name of self-preservation. "We can never be sure that a new idea will not seize either upon ourselves or upon our neighbors," Carl Jung wrote in "After the Catastrophe," and indeed "such ideas are often so strange, indeed so bizarre, that they fly in the face of reason."[7] In fact, Jung believed that these psychic epidemics spawn "a fanatical obsession, with the result that all dissenters no matter how well-meaning or reasonable they are, get burnt alive . . . or are disposed of in masses."[8] It is irrational ideas, not well-reasoned courses of action, that are most likely to suddenly and dangerously take hold in society. The emotion of the mob overtakes all else, and anything seems permissible.

This is the essence of totalitarianism.

America has never reached the true depths of mass delusion. Even the Covid era came nowhere close to the bloodthirsty, popular fever of Nazism or Soviet Communism. Because of this, comparing trends in America to the extreme mind-control regimes of the past can feel overblown. After all, we have far more freedom of speech and thought than the era of *The Gulag Archipelago*.

But we also know it's foolish to pretend it can't happen here. To do so would invite a resurrection of the atrocities that only mass delusion can sustain.

So to defend against tactics of mind control, we must understand how they have been abused in the past. We must come to grips with how malleable our minds really are when subjected to certain processes.

Truth be told, America faces two main risks of totalitarian mind control. The first is more remote: a brute-force elevation of the current political or technological apparatus into an instrument of total control. This could be through a trigger event like another global pandemic. Or it could be a political upheaval—perhaps a contested election leading to civil war. However the match is lit, there's no question that our government has the technical capacity and resources to go fully totalitarian (though it should be noted, around eighty million American gun owners stand in the way).

While this isn't going to happen tomorrow, we've been closer to this eventuality in recent years than at any time in living memory. There have been two era-defining events over the course of my adult life: 9/11 and the Covid pandemic. During both, Americans endured massive government overreach, including foreign wars instigated on false pretenses, the erection of a systematic spying system, pandemic lockdowns, vaccine mandates, the ascent of the deep state, and the trampling of constitutional rights.

Added to government overreach is the rise in hysterical, toxic partisan politics. A trend has grown where around half the country has little faith in the results of presidential elections. Millions go even further, believing with absolute certainty that an election was stolen, whether it be 2016, 2020, or another cycle (they may be right in at least one case). In particular, the Left has engaged in soft coup attempts like "Russia Collusion" and rigged prosecutions, all in an effort to destroy President Trump. That they failed does not lessen the treachery involved.

And a new precedent of endless political persecution has been set. The weaponization of law—particularly through bad-faith prosecutions of political opponents—is going to stay with us for generations. Locking up the leader of a political party in America has been normalized, at least in theory. From a historical perspective, that's exactly the kind of political overreach that could lead to spiraling bloodshed. And given the two nearly successful assassination attempts on then candidate Donald Trump (including one in which a bullet struck his ear), the likelihood of an Archduke Ferdinand moment must be taken seriously.

The Cult of Passivity

The second—and more likely—pathway to totalitarian-level mind control for America is more incrementalist.

Dr. Meerloo sounded the alarm bells almost seventy years ago that our soft-handed, sweets-addicted society was at risk for mind control—and that was when America was much less defined by abundance and convenience. "Silence, lonely relaxation—with alcohol, sweets, the television screen, or a murder mystery—may soothe the mind into a passivity that may gradually make it vulnerable to the seductive ideology of some feared enemy," Meerloo wrote.[9] He called this approach to life "the cult of passivity."[10]

Today it's not murder mysteries but the lazy, mind-numbing routines of endless Uber Eats, Oreos, and online streaming that leave an opening for mind control. During Covid, we saw that the masses are quite willing to obey quasi-totalitarian orders so long as they are fed and entertained. According to Dr. Meerloo, an overly comfortable society makes people more susceptible to mass delusion.

Additionally, there's the creeping totalitarianism of government programs with good intentions. Bureaucratized welfare can become an ongoing mechanism of conditioning that, over time, leads to a more blindly obedient society.

Case in point is recycling, which I've always found deeply

annoying and largely pointless. Most of the plastic that Americans are encouraged to recycle, for instance, ends up in landfills or sold overseas to developing countries where there is less waste control. The "recycled" plastic then finds its way to river systems and eventually out into the open ocean. But if you tell people recycling is a waste of time, they will often look at you like you're crazy (or immoral).

I've observed the most fastidious recyclers don't care what the results are, even when I tell them. They've internalized the message that good people recycle, bad people don't, and that's all that matters to them. This may remind you of your neighbor who never watches Fox News but holds a deranged hatred for the network because that's what he is told to do. Or perhaps your colleague who double-masked alone in his car for two years of Covid. All these are the ill effects of compliance conditioning.

Does recycling lead to totalitarianism? Of course not (despite what I tell my wife when it's time for me to separate the trash). But it's an example of forced compliance, through fines and propaganda, that becomes conditioned in the population. If you get in the habit of doing stupid things without asking why, it's less likely you will question new rules, even as they grow in importance. Remember, our Founding Fathers overthrew their government for daring to tax them without giving them representation in Parliament. But nowadays most Americans wouldn't even criticize the government when it locked them indoors for months on end. This transformation only happens with the slow creep of compliance—and it's a process that continues today.

Yes, we need a certain degree of trust in "consensus" for society to function smoothly, but the reasons should be clear. The proverbial "because I said so" is only acceptable for parents, never for the implementation of state power against free citizens.

What mass delusions does America face in the future? While it's impossible to say which is next, history shows us that crazy ideas can come back anytime. Just like the viral plagues of the body, viruses of the mind have a cyclical nature. In the aftermath of World War II, Carl Jung wrote that "just when people were congratulating themselves on having abolished [the belief in demons], it turned out that . . . tyrannical, obsessive, intoxicating ideas and delusions were abroad everywhere, and people began to believe the most absurd things, just as the possessed do."[11] His point—that Europe believed it had advanced past the carnage and mass delusions of World War I, only to fall into something much worse—must be taken seriously today.

As I see it, there has still been no meaningful accountability for the mass delusion of the Covid pandemic response. It was both horrifically ineffective and deeply authoritarian in a way that I would never have thought possible in America. There is an understandable desire to move on as a means to put the psychological trauma of it all behind us. But I am confident that much of the same madness would be repeated today if another pandemic hit.

The risks are even greater when considering the prospect of a pandemic with a higher fatality rate—something along the lines of the Spanish influenza of 1918. Given America's reaction to a virus that was, in essence, only substantially dangerous to the very old or very infirm, it's hard to imagine what totalitarianism we would accept in the face of something that kills anywhere from 3 to 5 percent of all those infected. Unless we come to grips with how American minds devolved into madness during the last pandemic, our response to the next one will be even more destructive and tyrannical.

But there is good news. While mass delusion can't be eliminated forever, it can be suppressed. The tools of conditioning, brainwashing, propaganda, and all the rest are powerful—especially when energized by new technologies. But we have free will, no matter what stratagems authoritarians deploy. While the end goal of totalitarian mind control is mass delusion, that in itself is, as Meerloo put it, "unadapted to reality."[12] It is simply not possible to turn humanity into obedient machines forever (at least not yet). The antidote to mass delusion—the innate desire for truth and freedom—exists within each and every one of us.

Not only that, but as the fundamental struggle for freedom is not new—we can draw on the wisdom of the past. In the sixteenth century, Étienne de La Boétie wrote in his *Discourse on Voluntary Servitude*:

> You can deliver yourselves if you try, not by taking action, but merely by willing to be free. Resolve to serve no more, and you are at once freed. I do not ask that you place hands upon the tyrant to topple him over, but simply that you support him no longer; then you will behold him, like a great Colossus whose pedestal has been pulled away, fall of his own weight and break in pieces.[13]

Right now, at this very moment, you possess all the tools needed to recognize and defeat every tactic to control your mind. You do not have to be a prisoner to mass delusions. This battle will never stop, but neither will your capacity for freedom.

Our minds and our souls are our greatest treasure. So fight for them. No matter what tricks or promises demons deploy, it is our duty to cherish and protect them.

Notes

Chapter I: Conditioning

1. "The Nobel Prize in Physiology or Medicine 1904," The Nobel Prize, accessed January 14, 2025, nobelprize.org/prizes/medicine/1904/summary.

2. Ivan Petrovich Pavlov, *Conditioned Reflexes: An Investigation of the Physiological Activity of the Cerebral Cortex* (Oxford University Press, 1927), 16.

3. Daniel P. Todes, *Ivan Pavlov: A Russian Life in Science* (Oxford University Press, 2014), 615.

4. Todes, *Ivan Pavlov*, 479.

5. Robert C. Tucker, "Stalin and the Uses of Psychology," US Air Force, Project Rand Research Memorandum, March 10, 1955, rand.org/content/dam/rand/pubs/research_memoranda/2006/RM1441.pdf.

6. Natalie Bettendorf and Jason Leopold, "Anthony Fauci's Emails Reveal the Pressure That Fell on One Man," *Buzzfeed News*, June 1, 2021, buzzfeednews.com/article/nataliebettendorf/fauci-emails-covid-response.

7. David Wallace-Wells, "Dr. Fauci Looks Back: 'Something Clearly Went Wrong,'" *New York Times Magazine*, April 24, 2023, nytimes.com/interactive/2023/04/24/magazine/dr-fauci-pandemic.html.

8. Tom Jefferson et al., "Physical Interventions to Interrupt or Reduce the Spread of Respiratory Viruses," *Cochrane Database of Systematic Reviews*, no. 1 (2023), cochranelibrary.com/cdsr/doi/10.1002/14651858 .CD006207.pub6/full.

9. Laurel Wamsley, "CDC Publishes—Then Withdraws—Guidance on Aerosol Spread of Coronavirus," NPR, September 21, 2020, npr.org /sections/coronavirus-live-updates/2020/09/21/915351325/cdc -publishes-then-withdraws-guidance-on-aerosol-spread-of-coronavirus.

10. Jose-Luis Jimenez, "COVID-19 Is Transmitted Through Aerosols. We Have Enough Evidence, Now It Is Time to Act," *Time*, August 25, 2020, https://time.com/5883081/covid-19-transmitted-aerosols.

11. National Center for Immunization and Respiratory Diseases (U.S.) Division of Viral Diseases, "Wearing Masks in Travel and Public Transportation Settings," Centers for Disease Control and Prevention, updated May 3, 2022, https://stacks.cdc.gov/view/cdc/117037.

12. Alondra Nelson, "Let's Clear the Air on COVID," *White House Office of Science and Technology Policy Blog*, March 23, 2022, whitehouse.gov /ostp/news-updates/2022/03/23/lets-clear-the-air-on-covid.

13. David Shepardson, Rajesh Kumar Singh, and Jeff Mason, "U.S. Will No Longer Enforce Mask Mandate on Airplanes, Trains After Court Ruling," Reuters, April 19, 2022, reuters.com/legal/government/us -judge-rules-mask-mandate-transport-unlawful-overturning-biden -effort-2022-04-18.

14. Dan Diamond, "In the Pandemic, We Were Told to Keep 6 Feet Apart. There's No Science to Support That," *Washington Post*, June 2, 2024, washingtonpost.com/health/2024/06/02/six-foot-rule -covid-no-science.

15. Jennifer L. Cadnum et al., "Real-World Evidence on the Effectiveness of Plexiglass Barriers in Reducing Aerosol Exposure," *Pathogens and*

Immunity 7, no. 2 (2022), paijournal.com/index.php/paijournal /article/view/533.

16. "Open Letter Advocating for an Anti-Racist Public Health Response to Demonstrations Against Systemic Injustice Occurring During the COVID-19 Pandemic," Google Drive document, updated June 6, 2020, https://drive.google.com/file/d/1Jyfn4Wd2i6bRi12ePghMHtX 3ys1b7K1A/view?pli=1.

17. Holmes Lybrand, "Fact Check: Four Times Walensky's Comments Were Out of Step with CDC Guidance," CNN, May 21, 2021, cnn .com/2021/05/21/politics/walensky-comments-cdc-guidance-fact -check/index.html.

18. Christina Maxouris, "A Covid-19 Outbreak in Provincetown Helped Change the CDC's Mask Guidance. Here's What Residents Learned and How They're Responding," CNN, updated August 2, 2021, cnn .com/2021/08/01/us/provincetown-outbreak-residents-response /index.html.

19. Alexander Bor, Frederik Jørgensen, and Michael Bang Petersen, "Discriminatory Attitudes Against Unvaccinated People During the Pandemic," *Nature* 613 (2023): 704, nature.com/articles/s41586 -022-05607-y.

20. Ingrid Hein, "Studies Reveal Negative Attitudes Toward the Unvaccinated," *MedPage Today*, December 21, 2022, medpagetoday .com/infectiousdisease/publichealth/102354.

21. David Leonhardt, "Covid's Partisan Errors," *New York Times Morning Newsletter*, March 18, 2021, nytimes.com/2021/03/18 /briefing/atlanta-shootings-kamala-harris-tax-deadline-2021 .html.

22. Johanna Alonso, "COVID-19 Vaccine Mandates Are Almost Gone," *Inside Higher Ed*, August 18, 2023, insidehighered.com/news/students

/physical-mental-health/2023/08/18/two-years-few-colleges
-still-require-covid-vaccines.

23. Michael Olufemi Sodipo, "Mitigating Radicalism in Northern
Nigeria," Africa Center for Strategic Studies, Africa Security Brief No.
26, August 31, 2013, https://africacenter.org/publication/mitigating
-radicalism-in-northern-nigeria.

24. Sodipo, "Mitigating Radicalism in Northern Nigeria."

Chapter 2: Menticide

1. Robert Conquest, *The Great Terror: A Reassessment* (Oxford University
Press, 2008), 109.

2. Conquest, *The Great Terror*, 109.

3. Conquest, *The Great Terror*, 109.

4. Conquest, *The Great Terror*, 121.

5. Conquest, *The Great Terror*, 123.

6. Conquest, *The Great Terror*, 122.

7. Joost Meerloo, *The Rape of the Mind: The Psychology of Thought
Control, Menticide, and Brainwashing* (World Publishing Company,
1956), 28, https://archive.org/details/rapeofmindpsycho0000meer
/page/28/mode/2up.

8. Meerloo, *The Rape of the Mind*, 91.

9. Meerloo, *The Rape of the Mind*, 90.

10. Meerloo, *The Rape of the Mind*, 91.

11. Meerloo, *The Rape of the Mind*, 91.

12. Meerloo, *The Rape of the Mind*, 91.

13. Meerloo, *The Rape of the Mind*, 92.

14. Meerloo, *The Rape of the Mind*, 28.

15. Meerloo, *The Rape of the Mind*, 49.

16. Meerloo, *The Rape of the Mind*, 140.

17. George Orwell, *1984* (Houghton Mifflin Harcourt, 1983), 274.

18. Katie Barnes, "Amid Protests, Penn Swimmer Lia Thomas Becomes First Known Transgender Athlete to Win Division I National Championship," ESPN, March 17, 2022, espn.com/college-sports /story/_/id/33529775/amid-protests-pennsylvania-swimmer-lia -thomas-becomes-first-known-transgender-athlete-win-division -national-championship.

19. Robert Sanchez, "'I Am Lia': The Trans Swimmer Dividing America Tells Her Story," *Sports Illustrated*, March 3, 2022, si.com/college /2022/03/03/lia-thomas-penn-swimmer-transgender-woman-daily -cover.

20. NPR (@NPR), "The international governing body for track and field will ban trans women athletes from elite women's competitions, citing a priority for fairness over inclusion, despite limited scientific research involving elite trans athletes," Twitter (now X), March 26, 2023, https://x.com/NPR/status/1640112232204759040.

21. Meimei Xu, "Biology Lecturer's Comments on Biological Sex Draw Backlash," *Harvard Crimson*, August 11, 2021, thecrimson.com /article/2021/8/11/biology-lecturer-gender-comments-backlash.

22. Xu, "Biology Lecturer's Comments on Biological Sex Draw Backlash."

23. Carole Hooven (@hoovlet), "For anyone contacted about 'mistakes' they have made in reporting/describing my case: in some instances this may be justified (e.g., I was not fired, the person who initially attacked me was not a DEI Dean or in a paid DEI position), but in others maybe not," X, December 16, 2023, https://twitter.com/hoovlet

/status/1736078907718193221?ref_src=twsrc%5Egoogle%7Ctwcamp
%5Eserp%7Ctwgr%5Etweet.

24. Stephen M. Lepore, "Seattle High Schooler FAILS Quiz Where He
Marked Only Women Can Get Pregnant and That All Men Have
Penises," *Daily Mail*, December 12, 2023, dailymail.co.uk/news
/article-12857739/Seattle-high-schooler-FAILS-quiz-marked-women
-pregnant-men-penises.html.

25. "Menstruation," TransHub, accessed January 14, 2025, transhub
.org.au.

26. The White House, "FACT SHEET: White House Honors
Transgender Day of Visibility," White House Briefing Room
statement, March 31, 2023, whitehouse.gov/briefing-room
/statements-releases/2023/03/31/fact-sheet-white-house-honors
-transgender-day-of-visibility.

27. The White House, "FACT SHEET: White House Honors
Transgender Day of Visibility."

28. Liam Stack, "Drag Queen Story Hour Continues Its Reign at
Libraries, Despite Backlash," *New York Times*, June 6, 2019, nytimes
.com/2019/06/06/us/drag-queen-story-hour.html.

29. Russell Falcon, "Dallas Drag Queen Event for Kids Sparks Outrage,
Defense," Nexstar Media Wire, June 7, 2022, https://thehill.com
/homenews/wire/3514357-dallas-drag-queen-event-for-kids-sparks
-outrage-defense/; Craig Monger, "Huntsville Drag Queen Teacher
Admits to 'Strategically,' 'Covertly' Placing LGBTQ+ Material in
Classroom," *1819 News*, December 12, 2022, https://1819news.com
/news/item/huntsville-drag-queen-teacher-admits-to-strategically-and
-covertly-placing-lgbtq-material-in-clasroom.

30. American Medical Association, "AMA to States: Stop Interfering in
Health Care of Transgender Children," press release, April 26, 2021,

ama-assn.org/press-center/press-releases/ama-states-stop-interfering
-health-care-transgender-children.

31. Cecilia Dhejne, Paul Lichtenstein, Marcus Boman, Anna L. V.
Johansson, Niklas Långström, and Mikael Landén, "Long-Term
Follow-Up of Transsexual Persons Undergoing Sex Reassignment
Surgery: Cohort Study in Sweden," *PLoS ONE* 6, no. 2 (2011), https://
journals.plos.org/plosone/article?id=10.1371/journal.pone.0016885.

32. Timmy Broderick, "Evidence Undermines 'Rapid Onset Gender
Dysphoria' Claims," *Scientific American*, August 24, 2023,
scientificamerican.com/article/evidence-undermines-rapid-onset
-gender-dysphoria-claims.

33. Brown University, "Updated: Brown Statements on Gender
Dysphoria Study," news release, March 19, 2019, brown.edu/news
/2019-03-19/gender.

34. Babak Dehghanpisheh, "Iraqi Prison Tries to Un-Brainwash Radical
Youth," *Newsweek*, August 8, 2007, newsweek.com/iraqi-prison
-tries-un-brainwash-radical-youth-99325.

35. Dehghanpisheh, "Iraqi Prison Tries to Un-Brainwash Radical
Youth."

Chapter 3: Brainwashing

1. *Oxford English Dictionary*, "assassin," accessed January 14, 2025,
oed.com/dictionary/assassin_n?tl=true&tab=etymology.

2. *Online Etymology Dictionary*, "kamikaze," accessed January 14, 2025,
etymonline.com/word/kamikaze.

3. Peter Edson, "New 'Rightist' Organizer," *Washington Daily*, March
1962, cia.gov/readingroom/docs/CIA-RDP75-00001R0003003
00019-2.pdf.

4. Edward Hunter, *Brainwashing: The Story of Men Who Defied It*

(Farrar, Straus and Cudahy, 1956), 3, https://archive.org/details /brainwashingstor00huntrich/page/n11/mode/2up.

5. Conrad C. Crane, "Korean War Biological Warfare Allegations Against the United States: A Playbook for the Current Crisis in Ukraine," United States Army War College Strategic Studies Institute information paper, March 11, 2022, https://press.armywarcollege .edu/cgi/viewcontent.cgi?article=1517&context=articles _editorials.

6. Milton Leitenberg, "False Allegations of U.S. Biological Weapons Use During the Korean War," in *Terrorism, War, or Disease? Unraveling the Use of Biological Weapons*, eds. Anne L. Clunan, Peter R. Lavoy, and Susan B. Martin (Stanford University Press, 2008), 121.

7. Leitenberg, "False Allegations of U.S. Biological Weapons Use During the Korean War," 130.

8. "A Barrier to Armistice: What to Do About Prisoners of War," Korean War Legacy Foundation, accessed January 14, 2025, https:// koreanwarlegacy.org/chapters/a-barrier-to-armistice-what-to-do -about-prisoners-of-war.

9. "The POW Experience," Korean War Legacy Foundation, accessed January 14, 2025, https://koreanwarlegacy.org/chapters/the-pow -experience.

10. Kim Guise, "Operation Swift Mercy and POW Supply," National WWII Museum, September 18, 2020, nationalww2museum.org/war /articles/operation-swift-mercy-and-pow-supply.

11. Lorraine Boissoneault, "The True Story of Brainwashing and How It Shaped America," *Smithsonian Magazine*, May 22, 2017, smithsonianmag.com/history/true-story-brainwashing-and-how -it-shaped-america-180963400.

12. Brendan McNally, "The Korean War Prisoner Who Never Came

Home," *New Yorker*, December 9, 2013, newyorker.com/news /news-desk/the-korean-war-prisoner-who-never-came-home.

13. Crane, "Korean War Biological Warfare Allegations."

14. Robert Jay Lifton, *Thought Reform and the Psychology of Totalism: A Study of "Brainwashing" in China* (University of North Carolina Press, 1961), 5, https://archive.org/details/thoughtreformpsy0000lift/page /20/mode/2up.

15. Lifton, *Thought Reform and the Psychology of Totalism*, 5.

16. Lifton, *Thought Reform and the Psychology of Totalism*, 13.

17. Lifton, *Thought Reform and the Psychology of Totalism*, 13.

18. Lifton, *Thought Reform and the Psychology of Totalism*, 5.

19. Lifton, *Thought Reform and the Psychology of Totalism*, 67.

20. Lifton, *Thought Reform and the Psychology of Totalism*, 23.

21. Lifton, *Thought Reform and the Psychology of Totalism*, 23.

22. Lifton, *Thought Reform and the Psychology of Totalism*, 75.

23. Lifton, *Thought Reform and the Psychology of Totalism*, 26.

24. Lifton, *Thought Reform and the Psychology of Totalism*, 26.

25. Lifton, *Thought Reform and the Psychology of Totalism*, 36.

26. Mao Yushi, "I'm Trying to Solve a Decades-Old Mystery: How Many People Were Killed by China's Great Famine?," *Washington Post*, September 1, 2014, washingtonpost.com/posteverything/wp/2014/09 /01/im-trying-to-solve-a-decades-old-mystery-how-many-people-were -killed-by-chinas-great-famine.

27. Robert Jay Lifton, *Destroying the World to Save It: Aum Shinrikyō, Apocalyptic Violence, and the New Global Terrorism* (Picador, 2000), 13, https://archive.org/details/destroyingworldt00robe/page/n7 /mode/2up.

28. Lifton, *Destroying the World to Save It*, 16.

29. Lifton, *Destroying the World to Save It*, 27.

30. Holly Fletcher, "Aum Shinrikyō," Council on Foreign Relations backgrounder, updated June 19, 2012, cfr.org/backgrounder/aum -shinrikyo.

31. Lifton, *Destroying the World*, 36.

32. Fletcher, "Aum Shinrikyō."

33. Lifton, *Destroying the World*, 14.

34. Lifton, *Destroying the World*, 25.

35. Lifton, *Destroying the World*, 26.

36. Stephen Kotkin, *Stalin: Paradoxes of Power, 1878–1928* (Penguin Books, 2015), 3.

37. Anita Pisch, *The Personality Cult of Stalin in Soviet Posters, 1929–1953* (Australian National University Press, 2016), 115.

38. Pisch, *The Personality Cult of Stalin in Soviet Posters, 1929–1953*, 115.

39. Joost Meerloo, *The Rape of the Mind: The Psychology of Thought Control, Menticide, and Brainwashing* (World Publishing Company, 1956), 123, https://archive.org/details/rapeofmindpsycho0000meer /page/28/mode/2up.

40. Meerloo, *The Rape of the Mind*, 120.

41. Anna Nemstova, "Russia's New Stalin Center Evokes Pride, and Revulsion," NBC News, May 17, 2021, nbcnews.com/news/world /russia-s-new-stalin-center-evokes-pride-revulsion-n1267521.

42. Meerloo, *The Rape of the Mind*, 148.

43. Lifton, *Thought Reform and the Psychology of Totalism*, 17.

44. Sarah Mizes-Tan, "Sacramento Will Require Government Meetings to Begin with Recognition of Indigenous and Tribal Land Rights," CapRadio, December 14, 2021, capradio.org/articles/2021/12/14 /sacramento-leaders-want-government-meetings-to-begin-with -acknowledgment-of-historical-indigenous-and-tribal-lands.

45. Caitlin O'Kane, "Police Officers Kneel in Solidarity with Protesters in Several U.S. Cities," CBS News, June 1, 2020, cbsnews.com/news /protesters-police-kneel-solidarity-george-floyd.

46. Christopher F. Rufo, "DEI Cult," *City Journal*, February 9, 2023, city-journal.org/article/dei-cult.

47. Rufo, "DEI Cult."

48. Rufo, "DEI Cult."

49. Brynn Tannehill, "Is Refusing to Date Trans People Transphobic?," *Advocate*, December 14, 2019, advocate.com/commentary/2019/12/14 /refusing-date-trans-people-transphobic.

Chapter 4: Weaponized Law

1. New York City Office of the Mayor, "Transcript: Mayor de Blasio Holds Media Availability," July 10, 2020, nyc.gov/office-of-the-mayor /news/511-20/transcript-mayor-de-blasio-holds-media-availability.

2. Valerie Pavilonis, "Fact Check: Thousands of Black Lives Matter Protesters Were Arrested in 2020," *USA Today*, February 22, 2022, usatoday.com/story/news/factcheck/2022/02/22/fact-check-thousands -black-lives-matter-protesters-arrested-2020/6816074001.

3. Craig Melvin (@craigmelvin), "This will guide our reporting in MN. 'While the situation on the ground in Minneapolis is fluid, and there has been violence, it is most accurate at this time to describe what is happening there as 'protests'—not riots,'" Twitter (now X),

May 28, 2020, https://x.com/craigmelvin/status/1266030830
473940993.

4. Joseph Wulfsohn, "MSNBC's Ali Velshi Says Situation Not 'Generally Speaking Unruly' While Standing Outside Burning Building," Fox News, May 29, 2020, foxnews.com/media/msnbc-anchor-says-minneapolis-carnage-is-mostly-a-protest-as-building-burns-behind-him.

5. Bay City News and Mandela Linder, "Group Breaks Off of Mostly Peaceful Protest, Vandalizes Police Station, Sets Courthouse on Fire," NBC Bay Area, July 25, 2020, nbcbayarea.com/news/local/east-bay/hundreds-join-in-mostly-peaceful-protest-in-oakland-saturday/2332703.

6. Brian Flood, "CNN Removes the Term 'Violent' from On-Air Graphic Describing Protests in Wisconsin," Fox News, August 25, 2020, foxnews.com/media/cnn-removes-violent-on-air-protests-kenosha-wisconsin.

7. Joseph Wulfsohn, "CNN Panned for On-Air Graphic Reading 'Fiery But Mostly Peaceful Protest' in Front of Kenosha Fire," Fox News, August 27, 2020, foxnews.com/media/cnn-panned-for-on-air-graphic-reading-fiery-but-mostly-peaceful-protest-in-front-of-kenosha-fire.

8. Arthur Koestler, *Darkness at Noon* (Modern Library, 1941), 75, https://archive.org/details/in.ernet.dli.2015.350530/page/n3/mode/2up.

9. George Orwell, *1984* (Houghton Mifflin Harcourt, 1983), 224.

10. Hannah Arendt, *The Origins of Totalitarianism* (Meridian Books, 1958), 462, https://archive.org/details/TheOriginsOfTotalitarianism/page/n481/mode/2up.

11. Alan E. Steinweis and Robert D. Rachlin, eds., *The Law in Nazi Germany: Ideology, Opportunism, and the Perversion of Justice*

(Berghahn Books, 2003), 80, https://dokumen.pub/the-law-in-nazi
-germany-ideology-opportunism-and-the-perversion-of-justice-97808
57457806-9780857457813-0857457802.html.

12. Steinweis and Rachlin, *The Law in Nazi Germany*, 93.

13. Steinweis and Rachlin, *The Law in Nazi Germany*, 93.

14. Steinweis and Rachlin, *The Law in Nazi Germany*, 93.

15. Steinweis and Rachlin, *The Law in Nazi Germany*, 91.

16. Steinweis and Rachlin, *The Law in Nazi Germany*, 139.

17. Steinweis and Rachlin, *The Law in Nazi Germany*, 40.

18. Steinweis and Rachlin, *The Law in Nazi Germany*, 39.

19. Steinweis and Rachlin, *The Law in Nazi Germany*, 92, 106.

20. Steinweis and Rachlin, *The Law in Nazi Germany*, 92.

21. Steinweis and Rachlin, *The Law in Nazi Germany*, 130.

22. Steinweis and Rachlin, *The Law in Nazi Germany*, 137.

23. Steinweis and Rachlin, *The Law in Nazi Germany*, 137.

24. Steinweis and Rachlin, *The Law in Nazi Germany*, 137.

25. Steinweis and Rachlin, *The Law in Nazi Germany*, 151.

26. Steinweis and Rachlin, *The Law in Nazi Germany*, 72.

27. Steinweis and Rachlin, *The Law in Nazi Germany*, 79.

28. Steinweis and Rachlin, *The Law in Nazi Germany*, 72–73.

29. Steinweis and Rachlin, *The Law in Nazi Germany*, 78.

30. Steinweis and Rachlin, *The Law in Nazi Germany*, 78.

31. NYPD CompStat Unit, "CompStat Citywide Report Covering the
Week 1/6/2025 Through 1/12/2025," Police Department City of New

York CompStat 32, no. 2 (2025), nyc.gov/assets/nypd/downloads/pdf /crime_statistics/cs-en-us-city.pdf.

32. Reuters, "Despite Recent Uptick, New York City Crime Down from Past Decades," April 13, 2022, reuters.com/world/us/despite-recent -uptick-new-york-city-crime-down-past-decades-2022-04-12.

33. Barack Obama, "Transcript: BET's Exclusive Interview with President Obama," interview by BET Staff, BET, December 12, 2014, bet.com /article/cqro4z/transcript-bet-s-exclusive-interview-with-president -obama.

34. Elahe Izadi, "Medical Examiner Rules Eric Garner's Death a Homicide, Says Police Chokehold Killed Him," *Washington Post*, August 1, 2014, washingtonpost.com/news/post-nation/wp/2014/08 /01/eric-garners-death-was-a-homicide-says-new-york-city-medical -examiner.

35. "Police Shootings Database," *Washington Post*, updated December 29, 2024, washingtonpost.com/graphics/investigations/police-shootings -database.

36. Eric Tucker, Michael Balsamo, and Chad Day, "Mueller Declares His Russia Report Did Not Exonerate Trump," Associated Press, May 29, 2019, https://apnews.com/article/donald-trump-ap-top-news-crime -politics-north-america-94323cfc164c4759ba6bf84ad2a46203.

37. Paul Bond, "Alvin Bragg's 'Soft on Crime' Policies Face Scrutiny as Manhattan DA Goes After Trump," *Newsweek*, March 21, 2023, newsweek.com/alvin-braggs-soft-crime-policies-face-scrutiny -manhattan-da-goes-after-trump-1789040.

38. Everett Rosenfeld, "FBI's Comey Says 'No Reasonable Prosecutor' Would Bring a Case Against Clinton for Emails," CNBC, July 5, 2016, cnbc.com/2016/07/05/fbi-director-james-comey-has-concluded -the-investigation-into-clintons-emails.html.

39. Kyle Cheney and Josh Gerstein, "Supreme Court Will Review Scope of Obstruction Law That Trump Is Charged with Breaking," *Politico*, December 13, 2023, politico.com/news/2023/12/13/supreme-court -will-review-scope-of-obstruction-law-that-trump-is-charging-with -breaking-00131514.

Chapter 5: Forced Phobia

1. Lorraine Adams and Ayesha Nasir, "Inside the Mind of the Times Square Bomber," *Guardian*, September 18, 2010, theguardian.com /world/2010/sep/19/times-square-bomber.

2. Adams and Nasir, "Inside the Mind of the Times Square Bomber."

3. Simone Kühn, Oisin Butler, Gerd Willmund, Ulrich Wesemann, Peter Zimmermann, and Jürgen Gallinat, "The Brain at War: Effects of Stress on Brain Structure in Soldiers Deployed to a War Zone," *Translational Psychiatry* 11, no. 1 (2021), nature.com/articles /s41398-021-01356-0.

4. Stanley Loomis, *Paris in the Terror* (Lippincott, 1964), 25–26.

5. John Kekes, "Why Robespierre Chose Terror," *City Journal*, Spring 2006, city-journal.org/article/why-robespierre-chose-terror.

6. Kekes, "Why Robespierre Chose Terror."

7. Simon Schama, *Citizens: A Chronicle of the French Revolution* (Knopf, 1989), 789.

8. Schama, *Citizens*, 789

9. Schama, *Citizens*, 791.

10. Schama, *Citizens*, 791.

11. Norman Hampson, *The Life and Opinions of Maximilien Robespierre* (Duckworth, 1974), 263.

12. James Matthew Thompson, *Robespierre*, 2 vols. (Appleton-Century, 1936), 2:208.

13. Loomis, *Paris in the Terror*, 403.

14. Loomis, *Paris in the Terror*, 403.

15. Kekes, "Why Robespierre Chose Terror."

16. Kekes, "Why Robespierre Chose Terror."

17. Steven Hassan, *Freedom of Mind: Helping Loved Ones Leave Controlling People, Cults and Beliefs* (Freedom of Mind Press, 2013), 123, https://avalonlibrary.net/ebooks/Steven%20Hassan%20-%20Freedom%20of%20Mind%20-%20Helping%20Loved%20Ones%20Leave%20Controlling%20People%2C%20Cults%20and%20Beliefs.pdf.

18. Andy Kessler, "Why Is Anxiety Rising?" *Wall Street Journal*, September 24, 2023, wsj.com/articles/why-is-anxiety-rising-covid-climate-social-politics-mental-health-5f033f53.

19. Thomas Malthus, *An Essay on the Principle of Population* (J. Johnson, 1978), 6, https://math.uchicago.edu/~shmuel/Modeling/Malthus,%20An%20essay%20on%20the%20principle%20of%20population.pdf.

20. Michael Shermer, "Why Malthus Is Still Wrong," *Scientific American*, May 1, 2016, scientificamerican.com/article/why-malthus-is-still-wrong.

21. Charles C. Mann, "The Book That Incited a Worldwide Fear of Overpopulation," *Smithsonian Magazine*, January 2018, smithsonianmag.com/innovation/book-incited-worldwide-fear-overpopulation-180967499.

22. Mann, "The Book That Incited a Worldwide Fear of Overpopulation."

23. Mann, "The Book That Incited a Worldwide Fear of Overpopulation."

24. NPR Staff, "Transcript: Greta Thunberg's Speech at the U.N. Climate Action Summit," NPR, September 23, 2019, npr.org/2019/09 /23/763452863/transcript-greta-thunbergs-speech-at-the-u-n-climate -action-summit.

25. "The Paris Agreement," United Nations Climate Change, accessed January 15, 2025, https://unfccc.int/process-and-meetings/the-paris -agreement.

26. James B. Ayres, "Scientist Predicts a New Ice Age by 21st Century," *Boston Globe*, April 16, 1970, newspapers.com/article/the-boston -globe-new-ice-age-forecast/36613964.

27. Letter from Brown University Department of Geological Science to President Richard M. Nixon, December 3, 1972, https://realclimate science.com/wp-content/uploads/2017/11/2017-11-01064204_shadow -763x1024.png.

28. "Another Ice Age?" *Time*, June 24, 1974, https://time.com /archive/6878023/another-ice-age/; Victor Cohn, "U.S. Scientist Sees New Ice Age Coming," *Washington Post*, July 9, 1971, https://web .archive.org/web/20160805020812/http://pqasb.pqarchiver.com /washingtonpost_historical/doc/148085303.html?FMT=ABS& FMTS=ABS:AI&type=historic&date=html+,+&author=By+Victor +Cohn|||||Washington+Post+Staff+Writer&pub=The+Washington +Post,+Times+Herald++(1959-1973)&desc=U.S.+Scientist+Sees+New +Ice+Age+Coming&pqatl=top_retrieves.

29. Walter Sullivan, "International Team of Specialists Finds No End in Sight to 30-Year Cooling Trend in Northern Hemisphere," *New York Times*, January 5, 1978, nytimes.com/1978/01/05/archives /international-team-of-specialists-finds-no-end-in-sight-to-30year .html.

30. Walter Sullivan, "Climatologists Are Warned North Pole Might Melt," *New York Times*, February 14, 1979, nytimes.com/1979/02/14

/archives/climatologists-are-warned-north-pole-might-melt-another
-projection.html.

31. Associated Press, "A Senior U.N. Environmental Official Says Entire
    Nations Could Be Wiped Off the Face of the Earth," June 29, 1989,
    https://apnews.com/article/bd45c372caf118ec99964ea547880cd0.

32. Steve Conner, "Don't Believe the Hype over Climate Headlines,"
    Independent, January 10, 2011, the-independent.com/climate-change
    /news/steve-connor-don-t-believe-the-hype-over-climate-headlines
    -2180195.html.

33. "Key Findings of the Pentagon," *Guardian*, February 22, 2004,
    theguardian.com/environment/2004/feb/22/usnews.theobserver1.

34. Tyler Stone, "Tucker Carlson: Anyone Who Was Paying Attention
    in America Understood That 'the Experts' Were Full of It," *RealClear
    Politics*, March 27, 2023, realclearpolitics.com/video/2023/03/17
    /tucker_carlson_anyone_who_was_paying_attention_in_america
    _understood_that_the_experts_were_full_of_it.html.

35. Stone, "Tucker Carlson: Anyone Who Was Paying Attention in
    America Understood That 'the Experts' Were Full of It."

36. Catharine Richert, "Kerry Claims the Arctic Will Be Ice-Free by
    Summer 2013," *PolitiFact*, September 2, 2009, politifact.com
    /factchecks/2009/sep/02/john-kerry/kerry-claims-arctic-will
    -be-ice-free-2013.

37. Steve Forbes, "The Case of Greta Thunberg's Deleted Tweet—What
    Alarmists Need to Hear," *Forbes*, July 14, 2023, forbes.com/sites
    /steveforbes/2023/07/14/the-case-of-greta-thunbergs-deleted
    -tweet—-what-alarmists-need-to-hear.

38. Caroline Hickman et al., "Climate Anxiety in Children and Young
    People and Their Beliefs About Government Responses to Climate
    Change: A Global Survey," *Lancet Planetary Health* 5, no. 12 (2021):

e863, thelancet.com/journals/lanplh/article/PIIS2542-5196(21)002
78-3/fulltext.

39. Sri Saahitya Uppalapati et al., "The Prevalence of Climate Change
    Psychological Distress Among American Adults," Yale Program on
    Climate Change Communication Climate Note, July 25, 2023,
    https://climatecommunication.yale.edu/publications/climate-change
    -psychological-distress-prevalence/#:~:text=Overall, 7% of American
    adults,change psychological distress (CCPD).

40. Office of the Surgeon General, "Our Epidemic of Loneliness and
    Isolation: The U.S. Surgeon General's Advisory on the Healing Effects
    of Social Connection and Community," US Department of Health
    and Human Services report, 2023, hhs.gov/sites/default/files/surgeon
    -general-social-connection-advisory.pdf.

41. Office of the Surgeon General, "Our Epidemic of Loneliness and
    Isolation."

42. Sylia Wilson and Nathalie M. Dumornay, "Rising Rates of Adolescent
    Depression in the United States: Challenges and Opportunities in the
    2020s," *Journal of Adolescent Health* 70, no. 3 (2022): 354–55,
    ncbi.nlm.nih.gov/pmc/articles/PMC8868033.

43. C. G. Jung, *Collected Works of C. G. Jung*, vol. 10, *Civilization in
    Transition* (Princeton University Press, 2014), 207.

44. Gustave Le Bon, *The Crowd: A Study of the Popular Mind*
    (Macmillan, 1896), 49, https://archive.org/details/le-bon-gustave.
    -the-crowd.-a-study-of-the-popular-mind-1896_202106/page/49
    /mode/2up.

45. Eric Hoffer, *The True Believer* (Harper & Row, 1951), 79, https://
    archive.org/details/truebeliever0000eric/page/74/mode/2up.

Notes

Chapter 6: Isolation

1. Robert D. Kaplan, *The Revenge of Geography: What the Map Tells Us About Coming Conflicts and the Battle Against Fate* (Random House Publishing Group, 2012), xvi.

2. Kaplan, *The Revenge of Geography*, xvi.

3. Michael Bond, "How Extreme Isolation Warps the Mind," BBC, May 13, 2014, bbc.com/future/article/20140514-how-extreme -isolation-warps-minds.

4. William Elliot Griffis. *Corea, the Hermit Nation* (Charles Scribner's Sons, 1888), loc.gov/item/04019932.

5. Matt Burgess, "The Bizarre Reality of Getting Online in North Korea," *Wired*, June 8, 2023, wired.com/story/internet-reality-north -korea.

6. Burgess, "The Bizarre Reality of Getting Online in North Korea."

7. Christopher Hitchens, "Visit to a Small Planet," *Vanity Fair*, June 2001, vanityfair.com/news/2001/01/hitchens-200101.

8. Leo Hickman, "Kim Jong-il: Ten Things You Never Knew," *Guardian*, December 19, 2011, theguardian.com/world/shortcuts /2011/dec/19/kim-jong-il-things-never-knew.

9. Zack Beauchamp, "Juche, the State Ideology That Makes North Koreans Revere Kim Jong Un, Explained," *Vox*, June 18, 2018, vox.com/world /2018/6/18/17441296/north-korea-propaganda-ideology-juche.

10. Beauchamp, "Juche, the State Ideology That Makes North Koreans Revere Kim Jong Un, Explained."

11. Yeonmi Park, "Leftists Are Making America More Like North Korea Every Day," interview by Buck Sexton, *Buck Sexton Show*, June 8, 2023, 39:29, audio, iheart.com/podcast/51-the-buck-sexton-show -27296753/episode/yeonmi-park-leftists-are-making-116869618.

12. Park, "Leftists Are Making America More Like North Korea Every Day."

13. Jodi Rudoren, Lynn Adario, and Tamir Elterman, "Syrian Refugees Struggle at Zaatari Camp," *New York Times*, accessed January 15, 2025, https://archive.nytimes.com/www.nytimes.com/interactive /2013/05/09/world/middleeast/zaatari.html.

14. "Ostracism: 'Cancel Culture' Ancient Greek-Style," *Sky History*, accessed January 15, 2025, history.co.uk/articles/ostracism-cancel -culture-ancient-greek-style.

15. "Jonestown," FBI History Famous Cases and Criminals, accessed January 15, 2025, fbi.gov/history/famous-cases/jonestown.

16. Todd Rose, *Collective Illusions: Conformity, Complicity, and the Science of Why We Make Bad Decisions* (Hachette, 2022), 47.

17. John Sweeney, "This Is What Happens When Scientologists Come After You . . . ," *Independent*, July 9, 2012, the-independent.com /voices/faith/this-is-what-happens-when-scientologists-come-after-you -7923556.html.

18. "What Does 'Suppressive Person' Mean?" Scientology, accessed January 15, 2025, scientology.org/faq/scientology-attitudes-and -practices/what-is-a-suppressive-person.html.

19. Lauren Kranc, "How NXIVM Seduced Hollywood Stars and America's Most Powerful Elite into a Barbaric 'Sex Cult,'" *Esquire*, October 17, 2022, esquire.com/entertainment/tv/a33658764/what-is -nxivm-sex-cult-celebrities-stars-the-vow-hbo-true-story.

20. Kranc, "How NXIVM Seduced Hollywood Stars and America's Most Powerful Elite into a Barbaric 'Sex Cult.'"

21. John M. Curtis and Mimi J. Curtis, "Factors Related to Susceptibility and Recruitment by Cults," *Psychological Reports* 73, no. 2 (1993), https://journals.sagepub.com/doi/10.2466/pr0.1993.73 .2.451.

22. Hannah Arendt, *The Origins of Totalitarianism* (Meridian Books, 1958), 225, https://archive.org/details/TheOriginsOfTotalitarianism/page/n481/mode/2up.

23. Arendt, *The Origins of Totalitarianism*, 407.

24. Arendt, *The Origins of Totalitarianism*, 317.

25. Arendt, *The Origins of Totalitarianism*, 317.

26. Arendt, *The Origins of Totalitarianism*, 356–57.

27. Robert Jay Lifton, *Thought Reform and the Psychology of Totalism* (University of North Carolina Press, 1961), 20, https://archive.org/details/thoughtreformpsy0000lift/page/20/mode/2up.

28. Lifton, *Thought Reform and the Psychology of Totalism*, 20.

29. Lifton, *Thought Reform and the Psychology of Totalism*, 20.

30. Tillman Durdin, "China Transformed by Elimination of 'Four Olds,'" *New York Times*, May 19, 1971, nytimes.com/1971/05/19/archives/china-transformed-by-elimination-of-four-olds.html.

31. "Columbus Circle Monument," Central Park Conservancy, accessed January 15, 2025, centralparknyc.org/locations/columbus-circle-monument.

32. Eric Hoffer, *The True Believer* (Harper & Row, 1951), 39, https://archive.org/details/truebeliever0000eric/page/74/mode/2up.

33. Anthony Leonardi, "Black Lives Matter 'What We Believe' Page That Includes Disrupting 'Nuclear Family Structure' Removed from Website," *Washington Examiner*, September 21, 2020, washingtonexaminer.com/news/1900774/black-lives-matter-what-we-believe-page-that-includes-disrupting-nuclear-family-structure-removed-from-website.

34. "The 1619 Project," *New York Times Magazine*, accessed January 15, 2025, nytimes.com/interactive/2019/08/14/magazine/1619-america -slavery.html.

Chapter 7: Identity Construction

1. Marc Santora and Adam Goldman, "Ahmad Khan Rahami Was Inspired by Bin Laden, Charges Say," *New York Times*, September 20, 2016, nytimes.com/2016/09/21/nyregion/ahmad-khan-rahami -suspect.html.

2. Santora and Goldman, "Ahmad Khan Rahami Was Inspired by Bin Laden, Charges Say."

3. Santora and Goldman, "Ahmad Khan Rahami Was Inspired by Bin Laden, Charges Say."

4. Michael Wilson, "Key Evidence in Chelsea Bombing Trial: Articles on Building Bombs," *New York Times*, October 3, 2017, nytimes.com /2017/10/03/nyregion/chelsea-bombing-trial.html.

5. Wilson, "Key Evidence in Chelsea Bombing Trial."

6. Marc Santora, Pir Zubair Shah, Joseph Goldstein, and Adam Goldman, "'Keep an Eye on Him,' Ahmad Khan Rahami's Father Says He Told F.B.I.," *New York Times*, September 22, 2016, nytimes .com/2016/09/23/nyregion/ahmad-khan-rahami-bombing .html.

7. Azmat Khan, "The Magazine That 'Inspired' the Boston Bombers," *Frontline*, April 30, 2013, pbs.org/wgbh/frontline/article/the -magazine-that-inspired-the-boston-bombers.

8. "San Bernardino Shooting: Who Were the Attackers?" BBC, December 11, 2015, bbc.com/news/world-us-canada -35004024.

9. Robert Jay Lifton, *Destroying the World to Save It* (Metropolitan Books, 1999), 3, https://archive.org/details/destroyingworldt0000lift_u0p4/page/n15/mode/2up.

10. Lifton, *Destroying the World to Save It*, 4.

11. Lifton, *Destroying the World to Save It*, 25.

12. Eric Hoffer, *The True Believer* (Harper & Row, 1951), 60, https://archive.org/details/truebeliever0000eric/page/74/mode/2up.

13. Joost Meerloo, *The Rape of the Mind* (World Publishing Company, 1956), 111, https://archive.org/details/rapeofmindpsycho0000meer/page/28/mode/2up.

14. Clive Martin, "The Seductive Power of Uniforms and Cult Dress Codes," CNN, June 6, 2018, cnn.com/style/article/seductive-power-of-uniforms-and-cult-dress/index.html.

15. Allison G. Smith, "How Radicalization to Terrorism Occurs in the United States: What Research Sponsored by the National Institute of Justice Tells Us," US Department of Justice, Office of Justice Programs, National Institute of Justice report, 2018, ojp.gov/pdffiles1/nij/250171.pdf.

16. *Diagnostic and Statistical Manual of Mental Disorders: DSM-5* (American Psychiatric Association, 2013), https://doi/book/10.1176/appi.books.9780890425596.

17. Smith, "How Radicalization to Terrorism Occurs," 10.

18. Smith, "How Radicalization to Terrorism Occurs," 11.

19. Meerloo, *The Rape of the Mind*, 88.

20. Joel Dimsdale, *Dark Persuasion: A History of Brainwashing from Pavlov to Social Media* (Yale University Press, 2021), 126.

21. Dimsdale, *Dark Persuasion*, 126.

22. Dimsdale, *Dark Persuasion*, 126.

23. Dimsdale, *Dark Persuasion*, 126.

24. Lifton, *Destroying the World*, 25.

25. Lifton, *Destroying the World*, 25.

26. Margaret Thaler Singer, *Cults in Our Midst: The Continuing Fight Against Their Hidden Menace* (Wiley, 2003), 114.

27. C. G. Jung, *The Symbolic Life: Miscellaneous Writings* (Princeton University Press, 1976), 571, https://archive.org/details/symboliclifemisc18jung/page/n3/mode/2up.

28. Gustave Le Bon, *The Crowd: A Study of the Popular Mind* (Macmillan, 1896), 10, https://archive.org/details/le-bon-gustave.-the-crowd.-a-study-of-the-popular-mind-1896_202106/page/49/mode/2up.

29. Le Bon, *The Crowd: A Study of the Popular Mind*.

30. Le Bon, *The Crowd: A Study of the Popular Mind*, xxi.

31. Mattias Desmet, *The Psychology of Totalitarianism* (Chelsea Green Publishing, 2022), 97.

32. Meerloo, *The Rape of the Mind*, 112.

33. Hoffer, *The True Believer*, 23.

34. Saul D. Alinsky, *Rules for Radicals: A Pragmatic Primer for Realistic Radicals* (Vintage Books, 1971), 121.

35. Alinsky, *Rules for Radicals*.

36. NEA Center for Social Justice, "White Supremacy Culture Resources," December 2020, nea.org/resource-library/white-supremacy-culture-resources.

37. Margo Edmunds, "Roadmap for Researchers: Navigating the Research

Process with an Equity Lens," AcademyHealth report, April 2024, https://academyhealth.org/sites/default/files/publication/%5Bfield
_date%3Acustom%3AY%5D-%5Bfield_date%3Acustom%3Am%5D
/ah_roadmap_2024_final.pdf.

38. Paul Szoldra, "Why the US Navy Wants Sailors to Read 'How to Be an Antiracist,'" *Task & Purpose*, June 23, 2021, https://taskandpur pose.com/news/us-navy-reading-list-how-to-be-an-antiracist.

39. Ibram X. Kendi, *Antiracist Baby* (Penguin Young Readers Group, 2020).

40. Stephanie Saul, "An Ambitious Antiracism Center Scales Back Amid Allegations of Poor Management," *New York Times*, September 23, 2023, nytimes.com/2023/09/23/us/ibram-x-kendi-antiracism-boston -university.html.

41. Ibram X. Kendi, "The Heartbeat of Racism Is Denial," *New York Times*, January 13, 2018, nytimes.com/2018/01/13/opinion/sunday /heartbeat-of-racism-denial.html.

42. Kendi, *Antiracist Baby*.

43. Kendi, "The Heartbeat of Racism."

44. Lilly Price, "Johns Hopkins Chief Diversity Officer Steps Down After Viral Backlash over 'Privilege' Definition," *Baltimore Sun*, March 6, 2024, baltimoresun.com/2024/03/06/johns-hopkins-diversity -officer.

45. Andrew Sullivan, "Is Intersectionality a Religion?" Intelligencer, *New York Magazine*, March 10, 2017, https://nymag.com/intelligencer /2017/03/is-intersectionality-a-religion.html.

Chapter 8: Propaganda

1. Daniel Stone, "New Space Station Photos Show North Korea at Night, Cloaked in Darkness," *National Geographic*, February 27, 2014,

nationalgeographic.com/pages/article/140226-north-korea-satellite
-photos-darkness-energy.

2. "Inmate Citizenship," US Federal Bureau of Prisons statistics report, updated January 11, 2025, bop.gov/about/statistics/statistics_inmate _citizenship.jsp.

3. US Department of Justice Office of Public Affairs, "Departments of Justice and Homeland Security Release Data on Incarcerated Aliens," press release, October 16, 2020, justice.gov/opa/pr/departments -justice-and-homeland-security-release-data-incarcerated-aliens.

4. Matthew Daly, "Pelosi Takes Hard Line on Paying for Trump's Border Wall," Associated Press, December 6, 2018, https://apnews .com/article/e3fd315c66554c22bfdf97710e0df711.

5. Dudley L. Poston, "Here's Why Trump's Border Wall Won't Work," Associated Press, January 5, 2019, https://apnews.com/article/lifestyle -travel-immigration-56d7094f0b554925abbd3d81f8ca74c8.

6. Pamela Kyle Crossley, "Walls Don't Work," *Foreign Policy*, January 3, 2019, https://foreignpolicy.com/2019/01/03/walls-dont-work.

7. Andrew R. Arthur, "Most Illegal Immigrants Do Not Qualify for US Asylum," Center for Immigration Studies, August 16, 2022, https:// cis.org/Oped/Most-illegal-immigrants-do-not-qualify-US-asylum.

8. Alisha Ebrahimji, Brynn Gingras, Gloria Pazmino, and John Miller, "At Least 7 Arrested, Accused of Attacking Police Officers Outside New York City Migrant Shelter," CNN, February 2, 2024, cnn.com /2024/02/01/us/police-attacked-new-york-outside-shelter/index.html.

9. Hailey Gomez, "NYC Resident Details Encounter with Migrants Begging 'Door to Door,' Says It's 'Madness,'" *Daily Caller*, February 17, 2024, https://dailycaller.com/2024/01/17/new-york-city-resident -encounter-migrants-begging-floyd-bennett-field-jesse-watters -raymond-maniscalco.

10. Michael Dorgan, "Times Square Shooting: Migrant, 15, Slapped with Attempted Murder Charges for Shooting at Police, Woman," Fox News, February 10, 2024, foxnews.com/us/times-square-shooting-migrant-15-slapped-attempted-murder-charges-shooting-police-woman.

11. "Key Findings About U.S. Immigrants," National Institute of Corrections, accessed January 16, 2025, https://info.nicic.gov/ces/domestic/population-demographics/key-findings-about-us-immigrants.

12. Victoria A. Velkoff and John M. Abowd, memorandum for Ron S. Jarmin, "Estimating the Undocumented Population by State for Use in Apportionment," US Census Bureau, March 27, 2020, https://www2.census.gov/about/policies/foia/records/2020-census-and-acs/20200327-memo-on-undocumented.pdf.

13. Michael Hoefer, Nancy Rytina, and Bryan C. Baker, "Estimates of the Unauthorized Immigrant Population Residing in the United States," US Department of Homeland Security Population Estimates report, February 2011, dhs.gov/xlibrary/assets/statistics/publications/ois_ill_pe_2010.pdf.

14. Merrill Matthews, "Matthews: Illegal Immigrants Double Under Biden—and That's Just the Start," *The Hill*, January 23, 2024, https://thehill.com/opinion/4423296-matthews-illegal-immigrants-double-under-biden-and-thats-just-the-start.

15. J. D. Tuccille, "Fix the Border Crisis by Making Legal Immigration Easier," *Reason*, December 1, 2023, https://reason.com/2023/12/01/fix-the-border-crisis-by-making-legal-immigration-easier.

16. Joost Meerloo, *The Rape of the Mind* (World Publishing Company, 1956), 100, https://archive.org/details/rapeofmindpsycho0000meer/page/28/mode/2up.

Notes

17. Ariane Knüsel, "Nazi Propaganda: The Radio," Swiss Educ educational handout, accessed January 16, 2025, swisseduc.ch /immersion/hist/ww2/propaganda/docs/radio.pdf.

18. Christoph Hasselbach, "Nazi Germany: Radio Propaganda Turns 90," Deutsche Welle, August 18, 2023, dw.com/en/nazi-germany-radio -propaganda-turns-90/a-66551137.

19. Farrell Evans, "8 Moments When Radio Helped Bring Americans Together," History.com, February 5, 2024, history.com/news/most -famous-historic-radio-broadcasts.

20. Sun Tzu, *The Art of War* (Wordsworth Reference, 1993), 101, https:// archive.org/details/suntzuartofwar0000taoh/page/100/mode/2up.

21. Mark Crispin Miller, introduction to *Propaganda*, by Edward Bernays (IG Publishing, 2005), 5, https://archive.org/details/propaganda -edward-l.-bernays/page/n5/mode/2up.

22. American Psychiatric Association, "New APA Poll Reveals That Americans Are Increasingly Anxious About Climate Change's Impact on Planet, Mental Health," news release, October 21, 2020, psychiatry.org/news-room/news-releases/climate-poll-2020.

23. Samantha Neal, "Views of Racism as a Major Problem Increase Sharply, Especially Among Democrats," Pew Research Center, August 29, 2017, pewresearch.org/short-reads/2017/08/29/views-of-racism -as-a-major-problem-increase-sharply-especially-among-democrats.

24. Ted Handler, J. Carlo Hojilla, Reshma Varghese, Whitney Wellenstein, Derek D. Satre, and Eve Zaritsky, "Trends in Referrals to a Pediatric Transgender Clinic," *Pediatrics* 144, no. 5 (2019), https:// pmc.ncbi.nlm.nih.gov/articles/PMC6855897.

25. Meerloo, *The Rape of the Mind*, 203.

26. Meerloo, *The Rape of the Mind*, 136.

27. Meerloo, *The Rape of the Mind*, 103.

28. Emilio J. Iasiello, "Russia's Improved Information Operations: From Georgia to Crimea," *Parameters* 47, no. 2 (2017): 53, https://press .armywarcollege.edu/cgi/viewcontent.cgi?article=2931&context =parameters.

29. Christopher Paul and Miriam Matthews, "The Russian 'Firehose of Falsehood' Propaganda Model," Rand Corporation Perspective report, July 11, 2016, rand.org/pubs/perspectives/PE198.html.

30. Paul and Matthews, "The Russian 'Firehose of Falsehood' Propaganda Model."

31. Meerloo, *The Rape of the Mind*, 47.

32. Meerloo, *The Rape of the Mind*, 102.

33. Meerloo, *The Rape of the Mind*, 99.

34. Lars Willnat, David H. Weaver, and Cleve Wilhoit, "The American Journalist Under Attack: Media, Trust & Democracy," Syracuse University, S. I. Newhouse School of Communications report, 2022, theamericanjournalist.org/_files/ugd/46a507_4fe1c4d6ec6d 4c229895282965258a7a.pdf.

35. Elon Musk (@elonmusk), "Massive public manipulation," Twitter (now X), May 9, 2023, https://twitter.com/elonmusk/status/1655968 899903418373.

36. The Rabbit Hole (@TheRabbitHole84), "If Legacy Media is going to shove bigotry porn down our throats it should at least do so in an honest manner so people have an accurate understanding of racial dynamics. Time and time again, Legacy Media has failed to do just that. H/T: @DavidRozado," Twitter (now X), May 9, 2023, https://twitter.com/TheRabbitHole84/status/16559682014220 12418.

37. The Rabbit Hole (@TheRabbitHole84), "If Legacy Media is going to shove bigotry porn down our throats."

38. Katie Reilly, "Read Hillary Clinton's 'Basket of Deplorables' Remarks About Donald Trump Supporters," *Time*, September 10, 2016, https://time.com/4486502/hillary-clinton-basket-of-deplorables-transcript.

39. Neal, "Views of Racism."

40. Meerloo, *The Rape of the Mind*, 47.

41. Meerloo, *The Rape of the Mind*, 46.

42. Meerloo, *The Rape of the Mind*, 47.

Conclusion: The Future of Mass Delusion

1. Thomas Barrabi, "Google Pauses 'Absurdly Woke' Gemini AI Chatbot's Image Tool After Backlash over Historically Inaccurate Pictures," *New York Post*, February 22, 2024, https://nypost.com/2024/02/22/business/google-pauses-absurdly-woke-gemini-ai-chatbots-image-tool-after-backlash-over-historically-inaccurate-pictures.

2. "Netflix Is Responsible for 15% of Global Internet Traffic Consumption," CNBCTV18, March 2, 2023, cnbctv18.com/photos/technology/netflix-is-responsible-for-15-of-global-internet-traffic-consumption-16080101.htm.

3. George P. Jan, "Radio Propaganda in Chinese Villages," *Asian Survey* 7, no. 5 (1967): 307, https://doi.org/10.2307/2642659.

4. "Neuralink," website homepage, accessed January 16, 2025, https://neuralink.com/#n1.

5. Reuters, "Neuralink's First Human Patient Able to Control Mouse Through Thinking, Musk Says," February 20, 2024, reuters.com/business/healthcare-pharmaceuticals/neuralinks-first-human-patient-able-control-mouse-through-thinking-musk-says-2024-02-20.

6. Reuters, "Musk's Neuralink Gets FDA's Breakthrough Device Tag for 'Blindsight' Implant," September 17, 2024, reuters.com/business /healthcare-pharmaceuticals/musks-neuralink-receives-fdas -breakthrough-device-tag-brain-implant-2024-09-17.

7. C. G. Jung, *Collected Works of C. G. Jung*, vol. 10, *Civilization in Transition* (Princeton University Press, 2014), 230.

8. Jung, *Collected Works of C. G. Jung*.

9. Joost Meerloo, *The Rape of the Mind* (World Publishing Company, 1956), 172, https://archive.org/details/rapeofmindpsycho0000meer /page/28/mode/2up.

10. Meerloo, *The Rape of the Mind*, 172.

11. Jung, *Collected Works*, 212.

12. Meerloo, *The Rape of the Mind*, 201.

13. Étienne de La Boétie, *The Discourse of Voluntary Servitude* (Unknown, 1576), https://oll.libertyfund.org/titles/kurz-the-discourse-of -voluntary-servitude.

Index

Index

Bragg, Alvin, 128
brain-computer interfaces (BCIs),
    243–44, 245–46
brainwashing, 68, 69–106
    in Communist China, 73–88,
        239–40
    confession and, 82, 83–85, 92, 101–2
    cults of personality and, 88–94
    cultural revolution in U.S. and,
        99–105
    reeducation and, 82, 85–87, 103–4
    Stalin and, 94–98
    suicidal militancy and, 69–73
    suicide bombers and, 68, 69–72, 73
    of U.S. POWs in Korean War, 75–79
Branch Davidians, 138
Brown, Michael, 126
bureaucratized welfare, 250–51

Catholic Church
    excommunication, isolation
        through, 169
    propaganda and, 220
Centers for Disease Control and
    Prevention (CDC), 28, 33
Chaunu, Pierre, 136
cheap fakes, 238–39
children, and transgenderism, 61–67
China, 12, 13
    brainwashing and, 73–88, 239–40
    collective guilt and, 100–101
    Cultural Revolution and, 11, 88,
        177–79
    internet in, 240
    isolation of atomized individuals and,
        176–78
    one-child policy in, 142–43
    prison cells, placement in
        intentionally crowded, 176–77

Christie, Chris, 130
Church of Fear, The (Sweeney), 172
classical conditioning, 19
Clay Travis and Buck Sexton Show, The
    (radio program), 10
climate change movement, 144–51
Clinton, Hillary, 128–29, 230
CNN, 145
collective guilt, 100–101
Collective Illusions (Rose), 171
Columbus monument, New York City,
    178–79
Comey, James, 128–29
conditional reflex, 19–21
conditioning, 17–37, 244
    Covid pandemic and, 17–18, 26–36
    masking/mask mandates and, 26–29
    Pavlov's conditional reflex and, 19–21
    physical stimuli, manipulation of, 26
    political mobilization and, 35
    science of, 19–26
    social distancing and, 29–32
    vaccination and, 33–35
confessions
    in brainwashing process, 82, 83–85,
        92, 101–2
    George Floyd riots and, 102
    land acknowledgment statements and,
        101–2
    menticide and, 42–47
confusion, as element of menticide, 55–56
Conquest, Robert, 43
Covid pandemic, 8, 9, 17–18, 26–36
    aerosol transmission spread of virus
        and, 28
    lack of accountability for response to,
        252–53
    masking/mask mandates and, 26–29
    natural immunity and, 34–35

Index

social distancing and, 29–32
vaccination and, 33–35
Crenshaw, Kimberlé, 206
The Crowd: A Study of the Popular Mind (Le Bon), 152, 197
cult of passivity, 250–52
cults
family separation and, 170–74
irrational phobia indoctrination and, 138–40, 152
isolation and, 170–74
process of indoctrination, 139
Cults in Our Midst (Singer), 196
cults of personality, 88–94
confessions and, 92
insecurity of followers and, 92
leader's ability to convey feelings of vitality and immortality and, 91–92
policing speech of followers and, 93
Shoko Asahara and Aum Shinrikyō cult, 89–91, 187–89
Stalin and, 94–97
Cultural Revolution, 11, 88, 177–79

Darkness at Noon (Koestler), 113
Dark Persuasion: A History of Brainwashing from Pavlov to Social Media (Dimsdale), 194–95
De Blasio, Bill, 109
Desmet, Mattias, 198
Destroying the World to Save It (Lifton), 89, 188
Diagnostic and Statistical Manual of Mental Disorders (DSM 5), 191–92
DiAngelo, Robin, 205–6
Dimsdale, Joel, 194–95
Discourse on Voluntary Servitude (La Boétie), 254
disinformation, 238

dissociative identity disorder, 191–92
diversity, equity, and inclusion (DEI), 101–4
Donovan, Joan, 226
drag queen performances, for children, 62–63
Durdin, Tillman, 177–78

Ehrlich, Paul, 142, 143
Enoch, Kenneth, 75–76
Essay on the Principle of Population (Malthus), 141
eugenics movement, 141–42
excommunication, 169
extinction anxiety, 140–44

fake news, 237–38
family separation, 170–74
Farook, Syed, 186
Fauci, Anthony, 26–27, 30, 35
fear, 133–40
French Revolution and, 134–37
ideals of ideology as justification for monstrous actions, 137
irrational phobia indoctrination and, 138–40, 152
trauma to brain resulting from, 133
firehose of falsehood. *See* lies, repetition of
Floyd, George, 8, 31
forced confessions. *See* confessions
forced phobia, 130, 131–54
climate catastrophism and, 144–51
durability and usefulness of, 151–54
extinction anxiety, weaponization of, 140–44
fear, consequences of, 133–40
Islamic radicalism and, 131–33
Foreign Policy, 212

Index

Index

"Is Refusing to Date Trans People Transphobic" (Tannehill), 104
Ivan the Terrible, 45–46

Jacobins, 136
January 6, 2021 protesters, 111, 129
Jasch, Hans-Christian, 116
Jean-Pierre, Karine, 238
jihadis/jihadism, 13
  hateful rhetoric and, 5–6
  Inspire and, 185–86
  in Iraq, 39–42
  in Nigeria, 1–6
  Rahami's bombing in NYC, 183–86
  suicide bombers, 68, 69–72, 73
Jimenez, Omar, 111
Jones, Jim, 138, 171–72, 196
Jonestown massacre of 1978, 170–74
Jung, Carl, 151–52, 198, 247, 252
Justice Case, 117–18

kamikaze, 72–73
Kekes, John, 135, 137
Kendi, Ibram X., 204
Kennedy, John F., 214
Kerry, John, 147–48, 153
Kessler, Andy, 140
Kim dynasty, 10–11, 13, 160–62
Kim Il Sung, 160, 161
Kim Jong Il, 160–61
Kim Jong Un, 160, 161
Koestler, Arthur, 113
Koltushi complex, 22
Korean War, 75–79
Kwangmyong, 240

La Boétie, Étienne de, 254
land acknowledgment statements, 101–2
language manipulation, 231–33

Le Bon, Gustave, 152, 197, 198
Left, in U.S.
  anti-border wall rhetoric and, 212
  antiracist identity construction and, 203–7
  attacks on U.S. history by, 178–79
  cheap fakes, denouncing truth as, 238–39
  crime, arguments regarding, 124
  fake news and disinformation accusations of, 237–38
  immigration narrative of, 214–17
  mass formation and, 196–97, 200–202
  menticide, use of, 58–67
  Obama's use of systemic racism claims, 124–27
  politicized and selective enforcement of law, 127–30
  propaganda of, 228–30
  "racist" as weaponized propaganda, 129–30
  soft coup attempts of, 249
  transgenderism, advancement of, 58–61, 65–67, 104–5
Lenin, Vladimir, 19, 21
Libby, I. Lewis, 129–30
liberation from totalitarian spell phase, of menticide, 51–52
lies, repetition of, 222–30
  indoctrination barrage and, 226–27
  media bias in U.S. and, 228–30
  number of countries with active cyber troop operations, 226
  Russian war propaganda and, 222–25
Lifton, Robert J., 79–80, 81, 82, 83–84, 87–89, 91–92, 93, 100–101, 176–77, 188–89, 195
Lincoln, Abraham, 180
Littman, Lisa, 65–66

Index

Index

Index